Low Attainers in Primary Mathematics

In this fascinating book, Jenny Houssart draws on close observation of children in lower mathematics sets in primary schools to investigate why some children opt out of mathematics at an early age. After introducing us to the children, the author addresses particular mathematical tasks in each chapter, including:

- mental work
- practical work
- written work
- calculators and computers
- assessment tasks.

Through stories and quotes we are shown how the children respond to specific tasks and see evidence of a range of difficulties that emerge as the children are working. Each chapter ends with discussions and implications for classroom practice.

Low Attainers in Primary Mathematics will be a useful resource for primary teachers, student teachers, SENCOs and teaching assistants who will all recognise these children from their own classrooms and draw insights from this highly readable book.

Jenny Houssart is a Research Fellow at the Centre for Mathematics Education at The Open University.

Low Attainers in Primary Mathematics

The whisperers and the maths fairy

Jenny Houssart

RoutledgeFalmer
Taylor & Francis Group

LONDON AND NEW YORK

First published 2004
by RoutledgeFalmer
11 New Fetter Lane, London EC4P 4EE

Simultaneously published in the USA and Canada
by RoutledgeFalmer
29 West 35th Street, New York, NY 10001

RoutledgeFalmer is an imprint of the Taylor & Francis Group

© 2004 Jenny Houssart

Typeset in Sabon by Wearset Ltd, Boldon, Tyne and Wear
Printed and bound in Great Britain by Biddles Ltd, Kings
Lynn

British Library Cataloguing in Publication Data
A catalogue record for this book is available from the British
Library

Library of Congress Cataloging in Publication Data
Houssart, Jenny.
  Low attainers in primary mathematics : the whisperers and
the maths fairy / Jenny Houssart
    p. cm.
  1. Mathematics–Study and teaching (Primary)–Research–
England. I. Title.
  QA135.6 .H68 2004
  372.7–dc22

                                        2003027013

ISBN 0-415-31553-0 (hb)
ISBN 0-415-31554-9 (pb)

Contents

Acknowledgements

The research in this book would not have been possible without the children, teachers and classroom assistants I worked alongside. My thanks go to them for allowing me to work with them and carry out my research and for helping me gain some insight into life in their classrooms. As usual, they remain anonymous and pseudonyms have been used throughout.

I would also like to thank others who have supported me in this research. In particular, colleagues at the Centre for Mathematics Education at the Open University, Milton Keynes, have listened to my ideas as the research progressed and encouraged me to develop them further. My partner, Richard Croucher, has supported my work throughout, practically, academically and emotionally. Our son Mark typed the manuscript as well as providing support in the face of technical problems.

The idea of the *whisperers* is developed from an article which appeared in *For the Learning of Mathematics* and I am grateful for permission to use and extend that article here. Some of the incidents in Chapter 8 are reprinted from the *Journal of Mathematical Behaviour*, vol. 21, no. 2, 2002, pp. 191–202 with permission from Elsevier. Other incidents used in this book have appeared in *Equals, TES Primary* and *Support for Learning*. I would like to thank the editors for allowing me to use them again here. Two test questions in Chapter 9 are reproduced with permission from the Qualifications and Curriculum Authority.

Introduction

Setting the scene

Alison, a teacher of 8- and 9-year-olds, was talking about what makes a good task in mathematics. She said 'with the bottom group, I'd say games, presentation of it as games ... yeah ... and the fact that it's not hard work. Bottom group really want to think they're there to enjoy themselves ... even at that ... I suppose that's quite young to be thinking that ... a bit worrying really. You do get a more work-orientated attitude I think with the brighter ones.'

The quote from Alison shown above played some part in leading me to research children in bottom sets in primary schools doing mathematics. This chapter deals with some general issues in order to set the scene. First of all, I explain the specific context in which the research arose. The next section deals with how the research was carried out, including research methods and some outline information about the schools and sets. Finally, this chapter looks forward to the rest of the book, saying something about the structure of the chapters and the messages contained.

How the research arose

Besides my long-standing interest in children with learning difficulties in mathematics, the research reported on here arose from two more immediate causes. The first was listening to teachers, such as Alison, as part of a project concerning tasks in primary mathematics. The original project started with individual semi-structured interviews with teachers about mathematics tasks. The quote above from Alison arose during one of these interviews. Alison had been asked to talk about what she felt made a good task for the children she taught. She worked in a school that operated a policy of 'setting', where children perceived to have similar levels of attainment were taught together. Alison taught the lowest of three sets, referring to them as the 'bottom group'. Other teachers also mentioned the set they taught when defining a good task. Teachers of bottom sets were more likely to talk about games and practical work. On the other hand, teachers of top sets were more likely to talk about the importance of providing challenging and interesting work. Similar points were raised in subsequent interviews (Houssart 2001a). For example, when teachers were shown commercially produced tasks and asked if they would use them with their current group, teachers of bottom sets were less likely to favour tasks perceived as 'open' or 'investigative'. Teachers of top sets, on the other hand, were less likely to design tasks around number equipment such as hundred squares or number lines which were perceived by many as being more appropriate for low attainers.

Following the interviews, the next stage of the project was to visit some classrooms and see the tasks in action. The responses to the interviews led me to become particularly interested in bottom sets.

The second immediate reason for my work was the possibility of getting the sort of high-quality access that such a project demands. I was fortunate that one of the bottom-set teachers involved in the interviews invited me to visit his classroom. This visit proved to be the start of a three-year project in which I paid regular visits to bottom-set classrooms. My initial interest was in the tasks the children were set, but this soon shifted to an interest in how they responded to the tasks. I tried to record and make sense of the difficulties children had and also became interested in the strengths that existed alongside the problems.

Carrying out the research

The schools and the sets

The primary schools researched were drawn from different local education authorities, but had certain things in common: they were large primary schools in towns and served mainly working-class areas. Their test results were below the national average, but were comparable to those of similar schools. The teaching of mathematics was rated as good by inspectors. One of the schools had a stable, mainly white population. Another had a wider ethnic mix and also had high pupil mobility. At this time schools were required to keep a register of pupils considered to have special educational needs and the number of pupils on the register was above the national average.

I worked with four sets of children, all of whom were considered to be in the lowest 25 per cent in their school as far as mathematics was concerned. Many were considered to have special needs. The issue of which children were in these sets is considered in more detail in the next chapter. The schools operated a policy of teaching children considered to be low attainers in fairly small sets. The smallest of the four sets I worked with contained twelve children; the largest of the four sets usually contained twenty-four children, though this varied. Three of the teachers were assisted by classroom assistants.

Approach to the data collection

Throughout the three years of classroom research, I used a participant observation approach, adopting a role similar to that of a classroom assistant, and this meant I was able to feel I was of some use and was able to develop a more intimate and informal relationship with those I was observing. My approach was ethnographic in that I sought to be close enough to the other participants to obtain a detailed picture of what was happening and to try to understand it.

Although I was happy to be of use in this role, I was clear from my initial entry into the classroom that I wanted to avoid the role of 'teacher' or 'expert'. This was because I wanted to see the children working on the mathematics they usually worked on, not something I had introduced in its place. While acknowledging that my presence must make some difference, I wished to minimise this. Thus I was anxious to present a low profile, behaving quietly and waiting for direction from the teacher about what to do. As incidents in this book show, I retained a low profile, though I did become involved in assisting children with the mathematics the teachers asked them to do. My awareness of the norms of the primary classroom acquired over years as a primary school teacher facilitated this. I believe that this approach assisted me in seeing much of the detail of life in the classrooms without influencing it too much.

Data collection

My main data was observational field notes as well as informal discussions with the teachers and classroom assistants. Note taking was minimal to start with but increased as the children and teachers got used to it. All were aware of my note taking though I tried not to make it too intrusive. The teachers occasionally made jokes about my notes, the children sometimes looked at the small notepad I used, occasionally asking if they could write on it. It is clearly not possible to record everything that happens in a classroom, but I tried to record the main events of every lesson, including as much detail as I could about the responses of the children I was near enough to observe and hear. It was always the case that I was happy to record 'ordinary' activities such as reciting tables or completing worksheets as well as anything more unusual.

Two other important aspects of my approach became clearer as the research developed. The first of these was that I became increasingly interested in informal mathematical activity initiated by the children as well as the formal activity planned by the teachers. Much of this informal activity consisted of children's comments about the mathematics, often made in a whisper. The second was that I recorded incidents even if they were very similar to previous incidents. This meant that if children were asked to do things like count in twos or answer questions about multiplying by four on several occasions, then I would record their responses whenever possible. As the research progressed, it became clear that, in many cases, when activities were repeated children did not necessarily respond in the same way.

How the questions developed

Initially I had only an outline idea of what I was looking for. My main focus was on children doing mathematics. I wanted to know what mathematics they were able to do and, if possible, how they went about it. I also wanted to see what their difficulties were. Given my initial focus on tasks, I wanted to see how the children responded to different mathematical tasks.

As my research developed, my situation presented opportunities which I regarded as relatively unusual and which I was keen to make full use of. The first was that my research was carried out in classrooms while children and adults were going about their normal business. Thus, I was in a position to observe learning in a classroom context, with all the practices, constraints, relationships and other factors involved. I was keen to try to understand how classroom factors impinged on children's performance. Also, weekly visits to each classroom for the duration of the school year gave me the opportunity to get to know individual children and try to build up a picture of their mathematics.

Two main themes developed. First, my records of informal mathematical comments initiated by the children led to the idea of *whispering*, which, in turn, led me to an awareness of the apparent mathematical strengths of some children. Second, my decision to record events similar to those I had already observed led me to recognise variability of performance. I refer to this as the *maths fairy*, for reasons that are explained in Chapter 2.

The more detailed information I gathered about individuals, the more aware I became of contradictions. Although the difficulties were immense, they existed together with strengths and successes. The atmosphere was largely positive and children and adults were generally working hard. Nevertheless, test scores and other formal assessments confirmed that the children were largely unsuccessful at mathematics. My observations tell a more complex and more positive story. Thus, the formal approaches to assessment did not satisfactorily capture the children's capabilities and reaffirmed their low estimate of their own abilities.

Overview of the book

Structure

Chapter 1 introduces some of the children who feature in the rest of the book. This is done mainly by describing their responses to various mathematical tasks. There is limited non-mathematical information about the children. This is limited for several reasons. The main reason is that I was given permission to research mathematical tasks and I wished to respect this and not ask repeated questions about other issues. Because I spent two years in each school, I inevitably did gather some informal information about children. I knew which children were often in trouble and sometimes aware of their difficulties outside school. I have respected the confidentiality of this information and not gone into detail. Nevertheless, there are places in the book where I have indicated that behaviour and personal circumstances may have affected the children's mathematical performance.

The rest of the book is organised according to type of task, using categories such as 'mental' and 'written'. This is partly for organisational reasons and I acknowledge that tasks can be classified in many other ways. There are some themes which run through the chapters and these are discussed and developed in the final chapter.

The chapters contain some reference to background reading in order to alert the reader to relevant issues and to similar work. In most cases, background sections include information about practices which were recommended at the time. This is done mainly to assist readers not familiar with the context. The central part of each chapter is concerned with incidents drawn from the classrooms. These are designed to look in detail at the children doing mathematics. This is followed by discussion, and most chapters end with classroom suggestions. The classroom suggestions are aimed mainly at those working in similar settings, either as teachers or classroom assistants. They start with suggestions for things that those working in classrooms might look and listen for. In doing this, they may be able to identify incidents similar to those I have described. The next set of suggestions is concerned with planning and teaching. They suggest ways in which adults might respond to difficulties or strengths they have identified. All the suggestions are no more than that. They are offered in the hope that some of them will be of help to some children. I do not offer any solutions which I claim will help all children, as a major finding of my research is that individual needs render this impossible. The problems are not amenable to simplistic or 'one size fits all' solutions.

Aim of the book

This book provides a detailed, complex and occasionally contradictory picture of children doing mathematics. I believe that it is necessary to include much of this detail since too much simplification will not present a true picture. Many of the individual incidents are open to more than one interpretation, and I would encourage readers to consider alternative explanations for these incidents and for those that occur in their own classrooms. The book suggests that many of the children perform quite differently in different situations. However, the circumstances leading to optimum performance differ for different children. For this reason, it seems that simplistic solutions are impossible but, rather, teachers can look for circumstances which may help individuals. For some children, the most positive information about their mathematical understanding came from the whispered comments which I recorded. This suggests that a more positive picture of children may emerge if attention is paid to their informal comments. It is possible that this picture might contradict the impression gained by looking at formal tasks completed by the same children.

Comparison of informal comments and performance on standard

tasks was not the only source of contradiction I found. For some children the way a task was presented, for example written or practical, was an important factor. Some inconsistencies proved hard to explain, however, as children sometimes responded differently to the same task or question presented in the same way, sometimes even on the same day. This calls into question assessment practices, which suggest that it is possible to fix and keep records of what children can and cannot do. It also challenges linear views of mathematics, suggesting that children cannot carry out a difficult task until they have mastered the previous step. In fact, the whole idea of mastery is questioned. The children I worked alongside rarely performed perfectly and consistently at anything. What they did do was show occasional flashes of insight, understanding and enthusiasm. I believe that encouraging and building on these qualities are likely to be more successful than a search for mastery, since it builds on success.

1 The children

It was my second week of working with children from the original Year 5 set. Within the set, the third of three sets, they were grouped by perceived ability into five groups. The teacher asked me to sit with one of these groups and to give particular help to one girl, Julie. He added that I would notice the difference between her and the child sitting the other side of me, Sean.

Introduction

The aim of this chapter is to introduce some of the children I worked alongside and to give a feel for their approach to mathematics. Subsequent chapters deal with particular types of mathematical task and most of the children introduced here are mentioned again in later chapters. I was often asked by the teachers to work with certain children and this chapter starts by introducing the group I worked with first. Some children from other classes are also introduced in order to indicate the types of children present. Before the children are introduced, the background reading section deals with some existing work on children in bottom sets as well as tackling the issue of labels and terminology. The chapter concludes that children in bottom sets can be different in many ways. It is difficult to make general statements that apply to all these children. Even to say that they are low attainers in mathematics is problematic for some children, who do not appear to have given a clear indication of their attainment.

Background

Who is in the bottom sets?

All forms of ability grouping carry the danger that certain groups of children might be over-represented in lower sets or streams. This issue is considered in a review of research by Sukhnandan and Lee (1998). They point to work which suggests that such sets or streams contain a disproportionately large number of children from working-class and ethnic minority backgrounds. Gender and season of birth are also said to influence placement of pupils. A further issue is whether children with challenging behaviour are sometimes put in bottom sets for this reason rather than on academic grounds. Research has suggested that both teachers and pupils believe this sometimes happens (Ireson and Hallam 2001). A further issue related to the composition of all sets is how similar the children in any set are likely to be. Some writers suggest that teachers commonly believe that children in given sets will all be very similar, but this is often far from the case (Boaler 1997).

Labels

This study is concerned with children who are in bottom sets, regardless of their reason for being there. It is difficult to talk about them as groups or to draw on relevant background reading without addressing the issue of labels. In some cases the teachers referred to these children as 'lower ability'. Most recent literature talks about 'low attainers' or 'low-attaining students', resisting the implication that success, or otherwise, at mathematics is inborn and unchangeable. At the time of the study, English schools were required to keep a register of pupils considered to have special educational needs. As Robbins (2000) suggests, there is likely to be considerable overlap between this group and those regarded as low attainers in mathematics. He goes on to say that the term 'special educational needs' is very general and can be thought to have limited value. A large-scale survey of the extent and type of special needs in English primary schools was carried out by Croll and Moses (2000). They found that the largest category consisted of pupils considered to have learning difficulties, followed by a group with emotional and behavioural difficulties. A much smaller group were identified as having health, sensory and physical difficulties. However, they also express reservations about the term 'special educational needs', suggesting that it is very difficult to define a point at which educational needs become special.

Low attainers in mathematics

Work on low attainers in mathematics has tried to both describe and explain low attainment. Descriptions of low-attaining pupils have tended to emphasise their diversity. Similarly, attempts at explanations have implied a breadth of possibilities. For example, Haylock (1991) talks about broad range and great variety in relation to children with low attainment in mathematics. He goes on to present case studies of individuals who show a complex combination of difficulties in understanding and engagement with the work. In an older study, Denvir *et al.* (1982) also draw on examples to illustrate the diversity of low attainers. They go on to assert that these children will not form a homogeneous group. In discussing reasons for low attainment, they suggest a range of possibilities. Some of these, they say, are beyond the control of the school, whereas others may be partly or directly under the school's control.

Evidence of attainment

The use of the phrase 'low attainers', while carrying fewer assumptions than 'low ability', is still problematic. It assumes that children have been offered opportunities to demonstrate their attainment and have done so. Problems are likely to arise if demonstration of attainment has been blocked by non-mathematical factors. For example, children with reading and writing difficulties may not show evidence of attainment on written tests. It is also possible that some children will not show evidence of attainment due to motivation or behaviour problems. Some groups of children present particular challenges as far as assessing attainment is concerned. Children who speak little or no English are unlikely to demonstrate their mathematical attainment if tasks are presented using spoken or written English. It is acknowledged by Hall (2001) that it is hard to assess the needs of bilingual pupils who may have special educational needs. She draws on the work of Wright (1991) in pointing out two possible errors. The first of these, 'false positive', involves diagnosing a learning difficulty when none is present. The other error, 'false negative', consists of failing to diagnose a learning difficulty. Thus, although it is crucial not to consider all bilingual children as having learning difficulties, it is important to acknowledge that some might.

There may also be some children who have not been provided with the opportunity to show their attainment if they arrive at a school after assessment has taken place and without evidence of prior attainment. The issue of mobility in schools has been the subject of recent concern (Dobson and Henthorne 1999). A study by Whitburn (2001) found lower levels of attainment in mathematics among mobile pupils as compared to stable pupils within the same school. A study looking at the effects of pupil mobility and what schools can do to mitigate these effects (OFSTED 2002) drew attention to the problems of assessing attainment. They acknowledged the difficulties for schools with high levels of mobility in induction and assessment. They also pointed out the impact of inadequate assessment on pupils. Some pupils interviewed for the study complained either that they had done work before or that they did not know what was going on. The study acknowledged the complexity of the relationship between attainment and mobility. They say this is partly because pupil mobility often occurs alongside other factors such as disrupted family life.

Contemporary advice

My research was carried out at a time when a large-scale national initiative, known as the National Numeracy Strategy, was being introduced in English primary schools. Documentation associated with the strategy (DfEE 1999a) offers advice to teachers about pupils with particular needs, including special educational needs. The main message is that as many children as possible should be included in the daily mathematics lesson. There is a push towards including all or most pupils rather than planning individually or over-differentiating. Teachers are encouraged to adopt strategies to enable all pupils to be included. These include minimising written instructions and making use of number aids. The section on special educational needs points out that children who have problems with mathematics often but not always also have literacy problems. The needs of pupils with emotional or behavioural difficulties are also briefly mentioned. Further guidance was subsequently issued to assist teachers and classroom assistants working with pupils with specific needs (DfES 2001). This document is divided into five sections, each of which offers guidance for working with pupils with particular needs. The needs are: (1) dyslexia or discalculia; (2) autistic spectrum disorders; (3) speech and language difficulties; (4) hearing impairments; and (5) visual impairments.

In the classrooms

There was some variation between the four sets of children I worked with in terms of the perceived needs of the children in the set. At one extreme was a mixed-age class of 7–9-year-olds, which I shall call the special needs set. The children in this set represented approximately the lowest 10 per cent of the attainment range in mathematics and all

were considered to have special needs as far as mathematics was concerned. At the other extreme was a set of 8- and 9-year-old children in
the same school, which I will refer to as the lower set. This set contained approximately the lower 50 per cent of the attainment range
but with the lowest 10 per cent removed. However, because the
school had approximately 35 per cent of children considered to have
special needs, there were many such children in this set. When
working in the lower set, I almost always worked with the small
group of children considered to have the greatest difficulty. The other
two sets of children both consisted of 9- and 10-year-olds. They were
in the same school but I worked with them in different years. One set,
which I will call the original Year 5 set, consisted of approximately
the lowest 25 per cent of the attainment range in mathematics. For
the later Year 5 set, this changed to about 20 per cent (see Table 1.1).
Additional information is given in Table 1.2, including the ages and
names of children. Only the names of children mentioned in this book
are included and all the names used are pseudonyms.

The information in Tables 1.1 and 1.2 gives some idea of the formal
position and hopefully will help those working in other schools to get
a picture of how the situations I worked in compare to their own.
Nevertheless, this information says very little about what the children

Table 1.1 The schools and the sets

	School A		School B	
Context	New housing estate, large town		Established area, small town	
% with special needs	30		35	
Set	Original Y5 set	Later Y5 set	Special needs set	Lower set
Year group	Y5	Y5	Y3 and Y4	Y4
Age of children	9–10 yrs	9–10 yrs	7–9 yrs	8–9 yrs
Number of children	20	18	12	24
Attainment in maths	Lowest 25% of year group	Lowest 20% of year group	Lowest 10% of year group	Lower 50% of year group, excluding lowest 10%
Adults	Teacher and two classroom assistants	Teacher and one classroom assistant	Teacher and two classroom assistants	Teacher and occasional voluntary help

Table 1.2 The children taking part in the study

Set	Original Y5 set	Later Y5 set	Special needs set	Lower set
Year group	Y5	Y5	Y3 and Y4	Y4
Age group	9–10-year-olds	9–10-year-olds	7–9-year-olds	8–9-year-olds
Names	Julie	Penny	Claire	Damian
	Sean	Craig	Douglas	Miriam
	Erica	Bhati	Adam	Heidi
	Linda	Lauren	Michael	Julian
	Rosie	Nadeem	Damian	Tony
	Wesley	Natalie	Joe	Sarah
	Darren	Adrian	James	
	Pedro	Bryn	Kate	
	Nadia	Matthew	Seth	
	Jed	Lawrence	Neil	
	Rashina	Susan	Quam Nam	
		Ella	Ben	
		Bob		
		Anja		
		Christopher		
		Malcolm		
		Stacey		

were like and what kinds of difficulties they experienced. In reality, there were great differences in the children and in their approach to mathematics. The rest of this section is spent introducing some of the children in order to illustrate the variety.

The table in the corner

My first term of fieldwork was with a Year 5 set. At the teacher's request, I worked with a group of children who sat at the table in a corner of the room. The children in the room were in the bottom of three mathematics sets and within the set the teacher had grouped them according to 'ability'. The group I worked with were the middle of five groups within the set. There were five children in the group. The teacher had particularly requested that I work with one child, Julie:

> Julie
> It was soon clear why the teacher felt Julie needed support. She found some aspects of calculation quite difficult. For example, she worked slowly through a sheet about multiplying by 4 and

had problems with calculations in the context of shopping, being confused by the mixture of addition and subtraction. She also had some difficulty in writing difference as a subtraction when the smaller number was given first. Julie persevered with formal methods of calculation taught by the teacher. She seemed to favour methods which dealt with numbers digit by digit rather than holistically. Despite Julie's success with formal written tasks, I continued to notice difficulties with aspects of number. For example, one week I worked with Julie on an activity about giving change for £1. At one point Julie was counting on from 88p to £1. She counted to 89 and said she didn't know which number came next. I encouraged her to try and she suggested first 70, then 80.

I soon noticed the difference between Julie's approach to mathematics and that of Sean, who sat on the other side of me. The teacher's comments recorded at the start of this chapter show that he was aware of this difference too:

Sean

In the first two weeks I noticed Sean's confidence in mental calculation. He was one of the fastest in the class at completing the sheet about multiplying by 4. On one occasion he fell behind the rest of the table because he lost his pencil. On tasks involving column subtraction, I noticed that Sean's work did not include crossing out of digits, suggesting he was not using the decomposition method advocated by the teacher. One task which Sean had problems with involved drawing a chart. The children had a chart on a piece of paper but had to copy this into their maths books. Sean did make an attempt to draw a chart but gave up when the columns turned out the wrong size. Sean sometimes made a point of saying that he found the work easy, and he seemed reluctant to seek or accept help. However, over the weeks he did start chatting to me, especially when I first arrived in the room before the lesson started. Sometimes during activities, he made comments in a whisper. These may or may not have been aimed at me but he did not seem to require a response. These comments or whispers became a regular part of mathematics lessons.

Although I continued to sit between Julie and Sean, I slowly got to know the other children at the table. Erica, who sat opposite me, was new to the school that term, having just arrived in the country. She was known by an English name but was of Chinese appearance and we later discovered that she had recently attended school in Singapore:

Erica
Erica spoke almost no English when she arrived, though it was encouraging to see how quickly she made progress with the language. However, she could do some of the mathematics, though this depended how it was presented. Worksheets involving computation only were unproblematic for Erica. She completed these sheets with a speed that particularly impressed Sean, who drew my attention to it. For example, she had no difficulties with a sheet involving subtraction of four-digit numbers. She did not cross the digits out but worked from right to left and completed calculations quickly and accurately. On the other hand, she was greatly slowed down by complex instructions, either spoken or written. One week the children were given a sheet headed 'sale', which started with a picture of a shop window full of priced items followed by word problems. Erica was at a loss to cope with the sheet until Rosie, the girl next to her, intervened. 'It's easy,' Rosie explained. 'If it's got the word "cost" in it, you add the numbers up. If it's got the word "left", then it's a take-away.'

The two other children on the table were called Rosie and Linda. Rosie sat between Erica and Sean. She seemed to cope reasonably well with the mathematics presented, though I never got to know her in any depth. After a few weeks, her attendance became intermittent. Around Christmas she disappeared altogether, although it was not clear when she officially left the school. The fifth child on the table was Linda, who sat on the other side of Erica:

Linda
Over the weeks, Linda started requesting my help on occasions, especially when worksheets had just been given out. She showed some anxiety about whether she knew what to do and whether she was doing what the teacher wanted. Once, when the teacher used the expression 'find the sum', Linda turned to me and said 'Miss, is it an add or a take-away?' She also expressed anxiety about non-mathematical aspects of the tasks such as whether they should work in pen or pencil and which way round they should have the paper.

After a term working on the corner table, I was able to reflect on the different mathematical needs and strengths of the five children. They had already been set by ability and were ability grouped within the set. It might seem reasonable to assume that such an arrangement should lead to a group of children who are similar mathematically. In fact, this was far from the case. Julie certainly had problems with mathematics, as did Linda. Sean's problems seemed to be of a different type. Erica could do mathematics presented in certain ways but was hampered by instructions given in English. Rosie was hampered mostly, it seemed, by intermittent attendance. Reflecting on the strengths and weaknesses of these five children led me to think about who ended up in bottom sets and why. In particular, there is a question about whether all children placed in bottom sets can reasonably be described as low attainers in mathematics.

The other children

As my fieldwork continued, I met other children who, like Sean, seemed adept at mental calculation but performed less well at written tasks. There were also others like Julie, who seemed to prefer formal written work to mental calculation. Three of the four sets I worked in contained children for whom English was not their first language, some, like Erica, in the very early stages of learning it. Children who were low in confidence, like Linda, were to be found in all four sets. The first school I worked in had relatively high pupil mobility. It contained sudden leavers like Rosie and children who appeared part-way through the year like Penny, who is introduced below. Another mid-year arrival in the same set as Penny was Craig, who had been moved down from a higher set:

Penny
Penny joined the school just before Christmas, having recently attended other schools in the area at which she was unhappy. Watching Penny over the next few months led me to believe she was still unhappy. I noticed plenty of negative body language such as pointedly leaning back on her chair. In one lesson, the teacher was demonstrating multiplication of two-digit by single-digit numbers on the board and was picking children to come to the board and help. Most children were sitting up straight in a very artificial way presumably in order to be chosen. Penny was still leaning back in her seat. A bit later, the teacher tried to draw

Penny into the conversation. He wrote a multiplication on the board in vertical format, 14×10. He asked Penny to explain how to do it. She said, '4 times nothing, which is nothing, er, 4, then 1 times 1 is 2.' Perhaps sensing that her answer was not going to be accepted, she added, 'That's the way *I* do it,' with emphasis on the 'I'. Over the year, Penny's attitude to mathematics varied. There were occasions when she started to show an interest in the ideas being discussed. This often occurred when the work became more difficult or puzzling. I did not work next to Penny until the last few weeks of the school year. When I did work with her, I realised that she had difficulty with formal methods of calculation, often misapplying algorithms she had once been taught and arriving at impossible answers.

Another child joining us midway through the year was Craig. Craig was originally in the third of the four sets. On one of my occasional visits to this set, I noticed that Craig sometimes behaved in a challenging way. As the year progressed, my impression was that this became more of a problem and eventually Craig was moved into the bottom set, joining us just after half-way through the year:

Craig
Craig's behaviour continued to vary, though the teacher worked hard to engage him in the mathematics. Sometimes, this was successful. For example, in one lesson the teacher used a number stick. This was new to his set but had been used by Craig's previous teacher. After straightforward activities such as counting in twos, the teacher suggested starting at 500 and counting in tens. Craig was one of only two children in the room who joined in the count. On another occasion, the children were asked to complete a worksheet, which involved adding twos and multiplying by 2. Due to disruptive behaviour, Craig was asked to leave the room. Soon after he had gone, the other children on his table pointed out that he had defaced the worksheet by making holes in it. These two incidents suggest that Craig's behaviour may have been influenced by the task, with co-operation more likely on harder tasks. Sometimes Craig seemed disaffected by events outside the lesson. However, even on these occasions, variation of task brought a change in his behaviour.

In the first school, I did not work closely with those children felt to have the greatest difficulties, because they already worked alongside other adults. All sets did contain children who were officially recognised as having particular difficulties. In formal terms, these children had what was known as a statement of special educational needs. The first such child I worked alongside was James, at the second school:

James

James was in Year 4 and had a statement of special educational needs. He had moderate learning difficulties and co-ordination problems. He was supported by a learning support assistant, Mrs Carrington. James had difficulty with activities involving recording, though his teacher kept these to a minimum. He did not always participate in oral activities on the mat, for example, joining in with the tables tapes. He seemed to have particular difficulty in mental sessions, when he was asked to carry out additions by counting on, though he did seem to be able to get the answer using a different method. He did well at the graphing lesson, despite his physical difficulties. He worked well using computers and seemed fairly knowledgeable about using the Internet and about moving in and out of programs. He had some difficulty using money.

James was one of a small number of children who had a particular type of special need which was taken into account during mathematics lessons. In particular, the adults avoided work which involved too much recording or the need for small writing. However, he was encouraged to develop physical skills such as drawing shapes and graphs but with support. Perhaps one reason why his difficulties were taken account of was the presence of Mrs Carrington, the learning support assistant who worked alongside him. Unlike the teacher, Mrs Carrington had worked with James in the previous year and in other lessons. She was aware of his special needs but also made a point of trying to encourage him to progress and she was wary of working so closely with him that he did not have the opportunity to show independence.

James was in a mixed age class which also contained Year 3 children. One of the Year 3 children causing the adults most concern was Claire. Unlike James, she did not have a recognised and named difficulty. She did have a reputation for challenging behaviour and this made it difficult to assess to what extent she also had learning difficulties with mathematics:

Claire

Claire was in Year 3. At the beginning of the year she was one of two children causing the adults most concern. I noticed that she had particular difficulty during an early lesson on addition. She did not respond to an activity about finding the total number of dots on a domino, even given a domino with one dot on each side. The adults reported that she had similar difficulties with early subtraction activities. However, in the case of both addition and subtraction, she performed much better on formal written activities. She particularly enjoyed writing on the whiteboard. Sometimes, Claire came to maths lessons upset and needed coaxing to join in. There were also occasions when she was reluctant to do what the other children were doing or to abide by classroom rules. As a result of this, for part of the year Claire was on a behaviour plan which involved being awarded ticks when she was doing what she was supposed to be doing and crosses when she wasn't.

Discussion

Non-mathematical difficulties

As the above profiles illustrate, I met children with a variety of strengths and difficulties within the bottom sets. This is consistent with the views of those who suggest that low attainers in mathematics are a diverse group (Denvir *et al.* 1982; Haylock 1991). Even when the children were grouped within the set, there were marked differences within the group. Sometimes children in bottom maths sets exhibited non-mathematical difficulties. In some cases these children did not appear to have difficulties with the mathematics itself. Informal remarks from teachers suggested an acceptance of the fact that children might be in bottom sets because they spoke little English, were poor readers or misbehaved. Sometimes the situation was more complex. There were some children who appeared not to have illustrated their mathematical understanding through formal tasks over a fairly long period of time.

It is interesting to consider whether all the children I worked with in bottom sets were low attainers in mathematics. Certainly, none had shown themselves to be high attainers, but in some cases there was a question about whether they had had opportunities to show their attainment. This was particularly true for children such as Erica who spoke little English and for those like Penny who arrived in the middle of the year. The teachers were aware of these difficulties and they were sometimes a subject of discussion between the adults. In one set a girl called Bhati arrived at the beginning of the year speaking very little English. Like Erica, she showed some promise at mathematical tasks involving little language. After a few weeks there was discussion about Bhati prompted by the language support team. They considered that placement in the bottom set was not appropriate given her mathematical understanding and she was moved to another set.

In the case of Penny, the teacher agreed that it was difficult to know initially which set to put her in. She arrived with no records and still had none at the end of the school year. The teacher found this lack of information frustrating but felt that it could be deflating to place children in too high a set. He maintained that if Penny was wrongly placed, this would soon become clear as she completed all the work easily and correctly. In practice, this did not happen, either with Penny or with the others who arrived mid-year and were placed in bottom sets. This could of course be because they were correctly placed, but it is also worth considering whether some of these children did in fact simply perform at the level of the work they were given and may also have done so given harder work.

Mathematical difficulties

Some of the children had identifiable mathematical difficulties. For example, Julie demonstrated difficulties with understanding of number which are described in more detail elsewhere (Houssart 2001b). In the first term of the research, I was able to form a profile of Julie that showed her problems with number, demonstrated over a range of tasks. It proved much harder than I expected to form similar profiles of other children. One way of explaining this is to consider why Julie's difficulties were easier to assess. Julie was co-operative and hard-working. She seemed happy to work on the tasks set by the teacher and to share her views with me or with other adults. She was not hampered by language or writing problems and performed fairly consistently over the weeks. There therefore seemed to be few barriers to my finding out what Julie could and couldn't do.

Some children presenting such barriers did also have mathematical difficulties. One example of this was Penny. Her difficulties varied from Julie's in that they seemed to stem from faulty algorithms. Many of Penny's contributions suggested an understanding of mathematics and a desire to make sense of it, but this was not the case when she was using formal algorithms. She demonstrated little feel for the size of the correct answer and it was hard to get her to think about this. One possible interpretation of this is that Penny did in fact have deeper problems than it seemed in understanding number. Another interpretation is that she felt that formal algorithms were not supposed to make sense.

Inconsistent performance

With many children, I found it much harder than I had expected to make even simple statements about what they could or could not do mathematically. I found myself in sympathy with Hart (1996), who worked alongside children with writing difficulties and found that over a long period of time she saw the complexity of problems rather than the simplicity. In many cases, I observed children do similar tasks on different days with diverse results. Sometimes the same aspect of number was treated in different ways and this produced differences in performance. For example, Claire appeared able to add and subtract numbers as judged by written tasks but not as judged by oral and practical tasks. For many children, it was the other way round. Douglas, who will feature in later chapters, appeared to have great difficulties with both oral and written work, but performed relatively well when tasks involved computers or calculators.

It is possible that factors outside the classroom were partially responsible for inconsistencies in performance. Sometimes children came to mathematics lessons upset and apparently not in the mood to do anything. On a positive note, such children always did join in eventually. I found that their behaviour on such occasions was one clue to the types of mathematical task they preferred. For example, Claire joined back in one lesson when the task involved writing on the whiteboard. Penny and Craig both resumed co-operation on occasions when the tasks became more challenging. Another difficulty in observing children's responses to particular tasks was how to record their failure. Initially, I found myself writing things like 'didn't know the answer' or 'couldn't do' or 'wouldn't answer'. I soon realised that there was often little evidence to say whether it was a case of wouldn't or couldn't. I also realised that this was an on-going problem for the teachers and the classroom assistants I worked alongside.

Classroom suggestions

Opportunities to show attainment

My experiences suggest that it is important that all children be given the opportunity to demonstrate their mathematical attainment. This may appear a simplistic statement but can be a challenge, particularly in the case of bilingual pupils or mobile pupils. It is also important that pupils with reading and writing difficulties and with challenging behaviour are given opportunities to show their mathematical understanding. This may mean reducing the reading and writing involved in tasks. Another possibility is to vary the mode of presentation of tasks, as my findings suggest that some children perform better at mental tasks, some at written tasks, and some when technology is used. Another possibility is to include more challenging or open-ended tasks. My reason for suggesting this is that the only way of being sure that children cannot cope with something more complex is to occasionally give them the opportunity to do so.

Teaching diverse groups

However children are grouped, even within sets, diversity of needs and strengths is inevitable. The challenge for the teacher, therefore, is to try to cater for such a range. Presenting tasks in different ways as suggested in the last paragraph may go some way to addressing this problem. Providing tasks which can be answered in different ways or extended is another possibility. Some examples of 'elastic' tasks successfully used by the teachers I worked with are given in Chapter 8.

Another possible approach to providing for diversity of needs such as that demonstrated by the corner table is to encourage co-operation. Collectively, the children on this table had many difficulties but also many strengths. On the few occasions when they helped each other, this not only assisted those in difficulties, but enabled those helping to articulate their ideas. Another benefit of this approach was that it seemed to encourage those helping to feel that they did have something to offer.

The role of other adults

My observations suggest that other adults can have a crucial role in helping the teacher reach decisions about pupils. When it comes to children such as James and others with particular special needs, the classroom assistant can be a source of information and continuity. In the case of Bhati, the language support team played an important part in ensuring that mathematical attainment was considered despite language difficulties. Other instances in which other adults gave information to teachers involved parents. In the case of Miriam, her parents talked to the teacher about her particular needs and how these might be met. In the case of Damian, his parents raised the issue of whether he was showing his full potential in mathematics lessons. Miriam and Damian both feature in later chapters.

As a researcher, I soon realised that the role of classroom assistant was a very good one for learning about individual pupils. My conversations with the other classroom assistants confirmed that they saw a wealth of detail while working alongside the children. Where team work was well established between assistants and teacher, the sharing of information about children's progress was a regular part of their work. Given the pressures of time, it is not always easy for teachers and classroom assistants to have lengthy discussions about children. My observations suggest, however, that when time was found it was time well spent.

2 Maths talk

The teacher was being positive. He called out the names of various children and asked them to stand up. He then announced that all these children would be given a star because they hadn't shouted out. 'I haven't shouted out!' Penny shouted out indignantly. 'You were shouting out,' the teacher explained patiently. Penny grudgingly conceded that this was the case but added, 'I was trying to help.'

Introduction

This chapter is about spoken aspects of mathematics. It starts with a discussion of the place of language in the learning of mathematics, which is followed by incidents from the classrooms. These incidents show that the teachers gave priority to certain aspects of language in the teaching of mathematics, especially the introduction and use of vocabulary. The chapter draws on the talk about mathematics I heard in the classrooms. Although much of this talk was official, some of the most interesting things I heard were in unofficial talk initiated by the pupils. The main finding of the chapter is that such talk is often strongly mathematical. My findings suggest that children apparently breaking unwritten classroom rules by shouting out or by whispering comments are often making significant contributions to the mathematics.

Background

The place of language in learning mathematics

There are many ways in which spoken and written language can play a part in the learning of mathematics. This chapter will focus mainly on spoken language. Durkin (1991) considers that the role of language in mathematics education is crucial. He goes on to consider different aspects of language and mathematics. These include the language of counting and early number, language and meaning, word problems and discussion. He points out that language is vital for communication in mathematics lessons as well as considering the role of mathematical vocabulary. Pimm (1987) talks of children learning to speak like mathematicians. He suggests that this involves control over the 'mathematics register', which is about both using particular words and speaking in a particular way.

Vocabulary and definitions

One apparently straightforward aspect of mathematical language is the need for children to use and understand the appropriate vocabulary. In practice, this can be quite complicated. One reason for this is the fact that many words used in mathematics are also used in another sense in everyday language. Sometimes the words have a similar but more precise meaning in mathematics, sometimes the mathematical meaning is not close to the everyday meaning. This is referred to by Durkin and Shire (1991) as lexical ambiguity. They give many examples of ambiguous words commonly used in school mathematics. Some are apparently simple words such as face, leaves, table and difference. They go on to give examples where children have confused the mathematical and everyday meanings of these words.

In some aspects of mathematics, for example shape, use of appropriate vocabulary is closely tied to an understanding of definitions. Thus, it is not just a case of children learning the word but of this being accompanied by an understanding of what the word means. Sometimes this can be complicated by potential misconceptions about definitions. For example, children may not use the word 'square' to describe a shape where the base is not horizontal because they do not accept this as a square rather than because they have forgotten the word.

Patterns of classroom talk

It is acknowledged that discourse in primary mathematics classrooms can be limited and follow predictable patterns (Brissenden 1988). Instruction and explanation can be dominant features of classroom talk, often driven by the need to maintain institutional norms (Bauersfeld 1995). Pimm (1987) points out that pupils do not speak only in response to the teacher and he distinguishes between them talking for others and talking for themselves. Studies of the culture of mathematics classrooms assert that pupils generally become familiar with the unwritten rules controlling classroom discourse. Such rules are part of the customs and practices which develop in classrooms and are taken as the norm by the participants (Cobb and Yackel 1998; Voigt 1998).

Language in the National Numeracy Strategy

The National Numeracy Strategy acknowledges the importance of mathematical language in several ways. One of the four key principles underpinning the strategy is 'direct teaching and interactive oral work with the whole class and group' (DfEE 1999a). In expanding on what direct teaching might mean, suggestions given are: directing; instructing; demonstrating; explaining and illustrating; questioning and discussion; consolidating; evaluating pupils' responses and summarising. The document goes on to suggest that a typical lesson should start with oral work and mental calculation. One suggested aspect of this is use of a good range of open and closed questions. The next part of the lesson, the main teaching activity, also offers opportunities for oral work. Suggestions made include: developing vocabulary using correct notation and terms and learning new ones; involving pupils interactively through carefully planned questioning and highlighting the meaning of any new vocabulary, notation or terms and getting pupils to repeat these and use them in their discussions and written work. The final part of the typical lesson is known as the plenary. Many of the suggestions given include mathematical discussion. Some of these involve the teacher, such as summarising key facts, others involve the pupils, such as inviting them to present or explain work.

Suggestions for appropriate vocabulary are given in detail in the supplements of examples which make up the major part of the *The National Numeracy Strategy: Framework for Teaching Mathematics* (DfEE 1999a). In addition, there is a vocabulary booklet accompanying the numeracy strategy (DfEE 1999b). This booklet starts with brief guidance about the importance of mathematical vocabulary and the use of questioning. It also gives examples of closed questions and open questions. However, the bulk of the booklet is concerned with listing the words children should be introduced to or know in every school year from reception to Year 6.

In the classrooms

All the teachers put emphasis on the introduction and use of mathematical vocabulary. Words were frequently explained and the teachers often asked the children to remind them what particular words meant. The teachers also tried to vary their language using alternative words and often asked the children to suggest other words with a similar meaning. This occurred in the majority of lessons. In the sections that follow, I will discuss three particular aspects of mathematics in which language was stressed: calculation, number properties and shape. In all the sets, talk was usually initiated and controlled by the teacher. The pupils spoke mostly in answer to teacher questions and were expected to put their hands up and be given permission to speak. Generally, such rules were observed and the classrooms were orderly without being totally silent. I will use the term 'official talk' to refer to the open discussions initiated by or acknowledged by the teacher. There was also a certain amount of low-level talk on occasions. This was often carried out in whispers and was not aimed at everyone in the room. I will refer to this as 'unofficial talk'. This chapter will discuss various types of unofficial talk.

Language and calculation

All the teachers paid attention to the language associated with calculation. In particular, they introduced alternative words for mathematical operations. In one lesson about addition, the teacher started the lesson by collecting possible words and phrases on the blackboard. These were add, plus, increase, find the sum and find the total. Later in the year, this list was repeated with a matching list for subtraction which included subtract, decrease and take away. Teachers sometimes started lessons on a particular operation by asking for alternative words. This tactic met with limited success. The two examples below are drawn from the original Year 5 set. The first example occurred early in the first term. The second example happened twelve weeks later:

> The first part of the lesson was about what the teacher called the '4 times table'. Following this, the teacher asked for another word for 'times'. Eventually, he received the answers 'multiply' and 'multiplication' but this took some time.

The teacher started the lesson by asking the children another word for 'times'. The first answer offered was 'divide'. This was followed by 'shared'. Julie then suggested 'add' and finally Sean suggested 'multiplied'.

Similar incidents occurred in other sets. When children were asked for alternative words to describe mathematical operations, incorrect answers were common. It was hard to tell whether the children were offering answers which they thought were correct or whether they simply named all the operations they could think of, knowing the teacher would tell them when they hit on the right one.

One of the words used in connection with subtraction was 'difference'. This caused particular difficulties. The stories below are both drawn from the later Year 5 set. The second incident took place four weeks after the first one:

> During work on sequences, the teacher asked the question, 'What is the difference between 10 and 20?' This caused some confusion and the teacher explained that they were adding 10 in order to complete the sequence.

> The children were using hundred squares and had coloured in 30 and 27. Referring to these two numbers, the teacher asked, 'What is the difference?' One answer from Lauren was '27 hasn't got a 3 in it.' The teacher reworded the question using the phrase 'How much bigger?'

In another incident, drawn from the original Year 5 set, it was the child rather than the teacher who clarified the meaning of the word 'difference':

> The children were cutting and measuring straws. They then moved on to fill in a chart which was headed 'difference in length'. They had worked on a similar activity with the same title the day before. Julie had two straws underneath each other. One was 14 centimetres long and the other was 11 centimetres long. The teacher asked her the difference. Julie replied, 'That's shorter,' pointing at the 11-centimetre straw. The teacher responded, 'How much shorter?' Julie asked, 'Is it a take-away?'

Language and number properties

One aspect of mathematical language that frequently arose was connected with properties of number. This was particularly the case in the special needs set where activities often involved counting in twos, fives or tens and looking at the resulting numbers. The incidents below come from a lesson in April. Although counting had been a frequent activity throughout the year, the word 'multiple' had been introduced relatively recently:

> The lesson started with some work on number sequences. After that, the teacher asked them about the word 'multiple', which she had used the day before. She used the phrase 'Who can remember?' The children had apparent difficulty explaining what a multiple was, so the teacher rephrased the question. This time she said, 'Tell me a multiple of 2.' This proved easier and various children provided answers.

This is a good example of a teacher changing a question to make it easier. In fact, in her unofficial talk to the other adults, the teacher described the original question as 'a bit hard'. Changing the question showed that the children did remember what they had done the day before. It seemed that it was easier for them to give an example of something (in this case, multiple) than to explain the meaning of the word. The lesson continued with various children coming to the board and writing multiples:

> Adam came to the board and was asked to write a multiple of 5. After some prompting, he wrote 55, then 80. The teacher said that one of these was also a multiple of 10. Michael quickly put his hand up and answered '80'. The teacher praised this answer and asked him to write another multiple of 10 on the board. He wrote 56.

This incident was interesting in that Michael's enthusiasm to answer suggested that he understood. This was contradicted by the example he then gave. In fact, it was not uncommon for children to display apparent flashes of insight followed by apparent lack of understanding. This was sometimes discussed by the adults in the class, who speculated about whether it meant that the correct answers were lucky guesses or whether there was some other explanation. In the case above, the teacher helped Michael by using a hundred square to look at the multiples of 10 and to talk about what they end in. The issue of what multiples end in featured again at other points in the lesson:

> Seth came to the board and was asked to write a multiple of 2. He wrote 20. The teacher picked up on the fact that the number was a multiple of 2, a multiple of 5 and a multiple of 10.
> Later in the lesson the children had to complete a worksheet. One question involved putting rings round multiples of 2. I was on the same table as Seth and noticed that he had put a ring round 205. When I discussed this with him, he said that it did end in 2. Looking at other questions on his sheet, I noticed that he had ringed almost everything as a multiple of 10.

Seth seemed to have particular difficulty with the idea of multiples, despite being able to count in twos, fives and tens, and despite generally being one of the highest attainers in the group. The phrase 'ends in' seemed to confuse rather than help Seth. He seemed to have a different view about which end of the number was meant.

Language and shape

The use of appropriate language was closely tied into learning about shapes. Children were encouraged to learn both the names and the properties of shapes. My first visit to the special needs set came after half-term. Before the holidays, the children had been working on shapes and the teacher used part of this lesson for revision:

> The teacher started by asking children for names of shapes. The names given were circle, square, rectangle, triangle and hexagon, in that order. This list matched the tray of shapes that had been used before half-term and was used later in the lesson. For the next activity, the teacher would pick a shape from the tray and conceal it under her hands. She would then describe the shape and ask the children to guess what it was. She started with a rectangle. She described it as having four sides and opposite sides equal. Adam suggested parallelogram. There was some surprise at this answer from the adults. The teacher then added that the shape also had 'square corners'. Another child suggested it could be a square. The teacher repeated that opposite sides were equal but said that not all the sides were equal. Kate correctly guessed that the shape was a rectangle. The teacher now changed the

activity slightly by hiding a shape in her hands and showing it to one child only, who had to describe it to the others. With a little help, Kate described the shape that she had had a quick glance of. One of the children correctly guessed it was a square but Kate said no. The teacher said to her, 'It is', and Kate responded, 'You went like that' (indicating that the teacher was holding it diagonally). 'I thought it was a diamond.'

There were several interesting points in this part of the lesson. Kate demonstrated a common misconception in thinking that the square was no longer a square because of the angle it was held at. At other points in the discussion, children gave correct if predictable answers. For example, the names of shapes they gave exactly matched those that they had been taught and used. However, the activity provoked Adam to correctly suggest that a parallelogram had the properties given. In doing this, he demonstrated knowledge and understanding that he had not been taught as part of his mathematics lessons. The child who answered 'square' was also giving an answer that was perfectly consistent with the facts. This may have been prompted by the phrase 'square corners', or it may have recognised the fact that if opposite sides are equal, it is also possible for all sides to be equal.

Humour

Sometimes the teachers included an element of humour in their talk. Sometimes the humour consisted of associating mathematical words with other words. For example, subtract was associated with submarines on the grounds that submarines go down under the water and when you subtract something from a number, it goes down. Another example comes from a Year 5 lesson about angles:

> The lesson was about different types of angles. The teacher introduced the word 'acute' by explaining that an acute angle was the same shape as a nose. Thanking the girl who he had used to demonstrate this idea, he said, 'It's a cute nose on a cute face.'

Humour often seemed to be aimed at getting children to remember things as often the same joke was referred to again as a reminder. A frequent reminder as far as angles were concerned was that the term 'right angle' did not have a partner. This arose in a lesson about angles when I was present. The way the teacher dealt with this made it clear that it had been discussed in previous lessons:

During the lesson, Nadeem used the phrase 'left angle' despite frequent reminders. At this point, the teacher said he wanted to introduce the chorus girls. Penny and Natalie stood up happily and when the teacher said 'Altogether now', they responded by chanting, 'There's no such thing as a left angle.'

Another thing children often had to be reminded of was the need to put in units. One of the teachers used humorous remarks about elephants to remind the children of this:

> Damian had come to the whiteboard to convert an amount of money from pounds to pence. After a few attempts, he arrived at the correct answer of 250. He did not write in the units and the teacher reminded him by saying, 'Were they elephants?' Damian smiled and wrote p after the number on the board. The teacher smiled as well and said, 'Good. Now we all know what they are.' As Damian went back to his place on the mat, he added in a whisper, 'Potatoes.'

The whisperer

During my first year in the classroom, I came across many examples of unofficial talk. This talk was often carried out in a whisper and was usually from four boys whom I shall call 'the whisperers'. They were Sean, Wesley, Darren and Pedro. A few others in the class made similar contributions on occasions but these four made regular and unsolicited comments. In the course of the year, I recorded such comments, or whispers, in all but two lessons:

> During the block of work on fractions, two worksheets were given out and the children were asked to look first at the one starting with a rectangle. This caused some confusion as one sheet started with a circle and one with a square. In response to this, the teacher said, 'Do you know what a rectangle is?' He pointed to the sheet in question and one of the children said, 'But it's a square.' The teacher looked again at the sheet, admitted that it was a square and apologised for calling it a rectangle. As the teacher started to explain the sheet, one of the children sighed slightly and said in a whisper, 'Well, anyway, it *is* a rectangle.'

These four boys had several things in common. They all made only modest progress over the year, failing to realise the potential shown in their whispered comments. All four seemed to have some non-mathematical difficulties, including problems with reading and recording, which hampered their performance in written tasks. On the positive side, they all did reasonably well in mental arithmetic tests requiring them to write answers only. Incidents throughout the year confirmed that the boys were reluctant to use the procedures and algorithms introduced by the teacher. They showed a preference for working mentally and for using methods which dealt with numbers holistically, rather than digit by digit. The comments of the whisperers also suggest that they were able to link work introduced to ideas they had met before. They also showed an enthusiasm for extending ideas and saying what they noticed, even if this meant going beyond what the teacher had planned for the lesson.

The unofficial comments made by the whisperers fall into three main categories which are described in more detail elsewhere (Houssart 2001c). The first category arose when the whisperers had noticed or discovered something. This sometimes involved generalisations, such as asserting that all multiples of 6 are even or that all rectangles have four right angles. On other occasions, the comments were about ways of reaching answers, such as 'it's 2 more' when forming a sequence of odd numbers. Sometimes a more complex discovery had been made, such as Darren's realisation that three distinct digits could be arranged to make six different numbers.

The second category involved extending or supplementing ideas, which might involve adding something to an answer that had been given, or to what the teacher was saying. In many cases this involved simply moving on to the next question or part of the question, but it could also involve continuing apparent patterns or predicting what would happen next. For example, in a task which involved colouring answers on a hundred square, the numbers coloured already were 6, 12, 24, 18, 36. Sean whispered that he thought the next answer would be 30. In a place value activity the teacher asked for the next odd number after 319. Pedro answered 321 in a normal voice, but then continued the sequence 323, 325 . . . in a whisper.

The third category involved the whisperers pointing out errors or things they didn't like. This sometimes arose when other children were asked to write or draw on the board or to give answers to completed work. Usually the whisperers merely pointed out errors and inaccuracies under their breath, though sometimes they did this in a normal voice. In all of the instances I recorded, the whisperers were correct in their identification of errors. Sometimes the whisperers went beyond identification of errors and exhibited a feel for what is important and correct in mathematics. An example of this occurred during a lesson about fractions. The teacher had written $\frac{1}{2}$ and $\frac{1}{4}$ on the board and was talking about which is bigger. He pointed out that although 4 is bigger than 2, $\frac{1}{4}$ isn't bigger than $\frac{1}{2}$. He speculated about why this is and Julie put her hand up and said, 'Size doesn't matter.' Sean said in a whisper, 'Size *does* matter.' The following week Sean made a similar comment. The teacher was drawing the children's attention to the line in a fraction which he said is like the division symbol except for the dots. Nadia said, 'Dots aren't that important.' Sean whispered, 'They is.'

Examples of unofficial comments made by the whisperers will be given in most of the following chapters. Although I use the phrase 'the whisperers' to identify these four particular boys, examples will also occur of children in other classes who made whispered, unofficial comments.

Shouting out

I have referred to unofficial and unsolicited talk as whispering even though occasionally the whisperers repeated comments in louder voices and were heard by the teacher. However, there were also incidents where the unofficial talk was slightly different in that it was made in a loud voice and the children made it clear that they wanted their comments to be heard. Teachers usually referred to this as 'shouting out'.

One example of this is given at the start of this chapter. This incident is unusual in that it actually includes an explanation from the child about why they shouted out. Looking back over the notes for that lesson confirmed that Penny had made several unasked-for comments, as she often did. For example, when the teacher had used the word 'product', she remarked, 'Same as times.' This fits in with Penny's explanation that she was . . . trying to help.' She often acted as a sort of unofficial translator in the classroom, explaining the teacher's actions or paraphrasing mathematical terms.

Usually both shouting out and whispering came from children who were not averse to bending the unwritten classroom rules. There were occasional exceptions when children who normally abided by rules and put their hands up to speak suddenly made unsolicited comments. An example of this is Lauren and her interruption during a lesson about fractions:

> The teacher had drawn a rectangle on the board and then drew the diagonals [see Figure 2.1]. He explained that the sections of

the rectangle were quarters. At this point, Lauren shouted out, 'How could that be quarters?' She stood up and went uninvited to the blackboard and continued her explanation 'because that bit' (at this point she touched the triangle formed by the long side of the rectangle, marked a in Figure 2.1) 'is not equal to that bit' (here she touched the triangle formed by the short side of the rectangle, marked b in Figure 2.1). The teacher did not engage directly with the issue of whether or not the sections were equal, or the underlying issue of what equal means in this context. However, he did acknowledge Lauren's intervention by rubbing out the diagonals and dividing the rectangle into quarters using horizontal and vertical lines.

Those children who shouted out were engaging in mathematics like the whisperers. Their comments included additions, disagreement and things they had noticed. In addition, they also showed a desire to help, to be included and to be acknowledged. Thus, although breaking the classroom rules, their actions can be seen as positive in many ways.

Adult talk

Because the classrooms I worked in usually contained several adults, there was potential for another type of talk, that between adults. Like talk between children, this was sometimes open and official and sometimes whispered and less official. In one classroom in particular, talk between adults played an important role in assessment. This will be considered in Chapter 9 on assessment. Occasionally talk between adults was part of the classroom humour. Often few words were needed, sometimes none. For example, in the shouting out incident described at the start of this chapter, the teacher and I exchanged

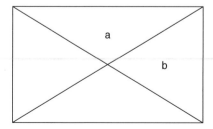

Figure 2.1 Diagram which led to Lauren's comments

looks and smiles when Penny shouted out, 'I wasn't shouting out!' though we did not say anything.

One issue that led to short whispered exchanges between adults was that of the *maths fairy*. This came about because the teacher was occasionally baffled by children's inability to do something they had done previously or sudden ability to do something apparently beyond them. The adult joke was that the maths fairy came to children at night, delivering mathematical powers. One example of this occurred in a lesson where the children surprised the adults by successfully reading large numbers in words and figures, including one thousand and one million. This led the teacher to remark that the maths fairy was 'bouncing around the room'. Usually the maths fairy was seen as a giver of mathematical power but occasionally she took it away. An example of this occurred during a lesson where the children had worked on several activities which involved counting on in fives. Neil was then asked to do '20 and 5 more' and he gave the answer '12'. This led the teacher to wonder, in an aside to the adults, whether the maths fairy had taken all his maths away.

Discussion

Mathematical vocabulary

There are some points that arose across the different classes. One of these is the emphasis put on language and the care taken to use varied vocabulary. A common occurrence was a kind of translation between common words such as 'times' and their more formal equivalents such as 'multiplication'. Switching between the two types of word was an official activity instigated by the teachers but also sometimes became an unofficial activity when the children translated words. This translation could be seen as moving in and out of the 'mathematics register', as discussed by Pimm (1987).

The teachers worked hard to encourage children to understand and use formal mathematics vocabulary. Direct attempts at this were not always successful. Children did not always respond well to requests to define a word or give an alternative word at the start of a lesson. However, when teachers started to use mathematical words, the response was slightly different. Children now seemed to see the need for alternatives and often engaged in 'translation' of terms themselves. Similarly, children unable to give definitions of words could often show their understanding once the activities started, perhaps by giving examples.

I can suggest two possible reasons why this might be the case. The first is that children may not see any great need to give alternatives for a word as an activity in its own right. However, when a task is presented using a mathematical word that they are unsure of, establishing the meaning of that word becomes an essential activity. Another explanation might be that use of vocabulary is hard to separate from understanding of concepts. As lessons progressed, children were able to develop their understanding of the ideas presented alongside the vocabulary being used. At the end of lessons, they seemed more confident in their understanding and were also often using the mathematical vocabulary themselves.

Whispering

One of the questions raised by the whisperers is why these boys made whispered comments, despite apparently having little effect. This raises the question of whether they were talking for others, or for themselves, a distinction drawn by Pimm (1987). In most cases they did not seem concerned that their comments were not heard by the teacher, though it is possible that they were talking for 'others' in the room, but not the teacher. They may have been whispering for each other. Responses to comments from the other whisperers were infrequent, but suggest they were able to see the value of each other's comments. It is also possible that Sean, who often sat next to me, was whispering to me in my role as a helper. He may have perceived me as less likely to judge than the teacher as well as knowing that I was unlikely to respond because the teacher was talking. Another possibility is that the whisperers were talking for themselves, trying to formulate their ideas.

Whether the boys were making comments for themselves or others, the comments provided evidence of unofficial mathematical activity which they were engaging in. It showed that they were taking opportunities to do some mathematics which matched their own view of the subject. Whispering may have aided their thought process. It also meant they were able to register their understanding and sometimes their dissent. Thus the whispering can be seen as having a dual function, partly for the benefit of the person making the comment and partly for any potential audience. The whisperers got ideas 'off their chest' by expressing them in a whisper, with the possibility that someone with a similar view might hear.

It could be argued that the whisperers were acting like mathematicians rather than mathematical failures. In their oral contributions the whisperers demonstrated features which some teachers associate with 'able mathematicians', such as trying to generalise and showing an interest in pattern (Watson 1996; Allebone 1998). In fact, the spontaneous behaviour of the whisperers is similar to the behaviour many mathematics educators see as desirable but difficult to elicit. For example, the art of asking questions is highly regarded in mathematics, with emphasis put on the type of questions likely to promote mathematical thinking (Watson and Mason 1998; Martino and Maher 1999). However, it seems that in the case of this particular group of children, mathematical statements were made without questions being asked.

Inconsistencies

Despite their demonstration of mathematical understanding and occasionally mathematical knowledge in advance of that expected by the teacher, the whisperers consistently performed in formal work at a level well below that expected for their age. One approach to this contradiction might be to suggest that there are obstacles preventing these children from showing their 'true ability'. Certainly, there is some evidence that non-mathematical difficulties hampered the completion of written tasks on which they were judged. Such difficulties included poor reading skills, slow recording skills and difficulty with organisation of work and materials. Another possibility is that the idea of 'mathematical ability' is a vast over-simplification. In particular, the experiences of the whisperers suggest that it is perfectly possible to possess supposed 'higher-order' skills such as the ability to generalise or extend ideas, without being accurate in the completion of worksheets.

One key issue arising from the whisperers but relevant to other children I worked with was that of inconsistencies. The whisperers showed apparent mathematical understanding in their whispered comments but not in their written work. Other children showed their strengths in different ways. Sometimes it was hard to explain or predict the circumstances in which children would perform well.

The maths fairy

The problem of inconsistencies raised by the whisperers was highlighted again when I worked in the class where the maths fairy was mentioned. Although this was presented as a shared joke among the group of adults, it actually highlighted an issue that was of genuine concern to them. They found it very hard to explain the inconsistencies in children's performances. This became an important strand of my research as I tried to log children's performance over the weeks looking for patterns and explanations. The phrase maths fairy often flashed through my head as I pondered discrepancies. Sometimes I was reasonably confident that I could explain these inconsistencies. On other occasions I could only offer explanations with an awareness that there were alternatives. There were occasions where I could not even offer an explanation. Examples of inconsistencies will be given in most of the following chapters, sometimes they will be accompanied by tentative explanations.

Classroom suggestions

Observing and listening

A lot can be learned by listening for the unofficial talk in classrooms. In particular, classroom assistants sitting with groups of children may have opportunities to hear such talk. The following categories may well be present:

- Children have noticed or discovered something.
- Children wish to extend or supplement ideas.
- Children have spotted something they disagree with or don't like.
- A child is 'translating' mathematical language to assist the rest of the class.

Planning and teaching

As well as listening for unofficial comments, teachers may wish to make changes to their planning and teaching which might encourage such comments. This could be done in several ways:

- allowing opportunities for small group discussion, perhaps with an adult present;
- pausing before moving on to a new activity and perhaps explicitly inviting comments, extensions or other examples;
- using the plenary for children to share what they have noticed or discovered.

Another issue for teachers is the introduction of mathematical vocabulary, including definitions or use of alternative words. This is often done at the start of a lesson but, in addition, teachers might like to consider the following:

- using mathematical words as part of a task and allowing children to discuss the meaning in context;
- asking children how they are going to tackle a task and responding in a way that links the child's language to mathematical language;
- discussing alternative words or definitions at the end of a lesson when children have had the opportunity to use the words and work on the related concepts.

3 Mental work

Damian and Heidi were chosen to go first on the game known as 'shoot-out'. The two children stood at the front and the idea was that they were given questions to answer with the first to answer correctly winning and the other being out. One question was 2×6. Damian gave the correct answer of 12 and Heidi was out. Damian's next two opponents were children who were usually much more successful at maths than him. Despite this, he was faster than both of them in providing the correct answer to 1×6, then 2×6. A fourth opponent was chosen and the teacher repeated the question 1×6. Damian gave the incorrect answer of 12 and was out.

Introduction

This chapter deals with mental mathematics, which was a very prominent issue at the time the study was carried out. As the background section indicates, it is far from clear what counts as mental mathematics. I have included counting, recall of facts and mental calculation in this chapter. Calculation and other number work based on number aids such as hundred squares are dealt with in the next chapter. Although all the teachers took the current emphasis on mental work very seriously, they actually interpreted it in different ways. This chapter shows their different approaches and some commonalities. In particular, all the teachers put emphasis on recall of facts, particularly multiplication facts. This chapter indicates that considering the time spent on this, children still had difficulty in recalling facts, especially in less than favourable circumstances. It was also very difficult to say categorically which number facts the children knew.

Background

Growth of interest in mental calculation in Britain

In the twenty years preceding this study, there has been a growing interest in and concern about mental mathematics in British primary schools. The importance of mental mathematics was one of the issues raised by the Cockcroft Report (Cockcroft 1982). The advent of the National Curriculum in 1989 presented another opportunity to reconsider the place of mental calculation (DES 1989). The statutory parts of the document said little about how calculations were to be carried out. However, part of the document called the 'Non Statutory Guidance' dealt with the issue of methods of calculation and was very positive about the place of mental calculation, stating that it should be seen as a first resort. This received some attention from the mathematics education community; for example, the Mathematics Association produced a publication about mental methods with the subtitle 'A First Resort' (Mathematical Association 1992). Despite this, reports written after the advent of the National Curriculum suggested a mixed picture as far as mental mathematics was concerned. Examples of promising practice in mental mathematics were found in some schools, while in others standard written methods of calculation still dominated (OFSTED 1993, 1994).

In the 1990s, there was growing concern about the performance of English schoolchildren in international mathematics tests. This led both to criticisms of teaching methods in England and comparison with other countries. One outcome of this was a call for more emphasis on mental mathematics in English primary schools. A quick result of these concerns was that a mental arithmetic test was introduced to accompany the written tests already taken by all 11-year-olds in England. The mental arithmetic test was introduced as a voluntary national pilot in 1997 and the vast majority of schools participated (QCA 1998a). As a result of the pilot, some changes were made to the format of the test which became statutory in 1998 and was retained in subsequent years. One feature of the mental tests is the use of time limits of either five, ten or fifteen seconds, enforced by the use of tape-recorded questions. The introduction of these tests inevitably put pressure on schools to spend more time on mental arithmetic. It could also be argued that they reinforced the view that mental arithmetic was about giving answers to test questions in a time limit.

Place of mental work in the National Numeracy Strategy

Another change in the status of mental arithmetic was brought about by the introduction of the National Numeracy Strategy in 1999. The documentation accompanying it outlines four key principles on which it is based, one of which is an emphasis on mental calculation (DfEE 1999a). Detailed information is given about what this might mean for children of different ages. This is reinforced in a separate booklet which deals with the teaching of mental calculation strategies (QCA 1999a). Another aspect of the strategy relevant to mental calculation is the suggested format of mathematics lessons. It is recommended that the first five to ten minutes of each lesson is spent on oral work and mental calculation. Advice is given about possible content for this part of the lesson. Suggestions include counting, recall of facts, working out new facts, and developing mental strategies. Other advice about the starter includes the exhortation to 'Get off to a clear start and maintain a brisk pace.'

What counts as mental?

The dividing line between mental and other activities is not clear. This issue is discussed by Harries and Spooner (2000), who talk about the difficulty in finding a clear definition of mental mathematics. They point out that an extreme view on this is that all mathematical activity is necessarily mental. Another point of view is put forward by Askew (2001) who prefers to make the distinction between strategic and procedural calculation. Strategic calculation involves varying the method according to the numbers involved by using a range of strategies which are often mental. Procedural calculation, on the other hand, involves using the same method of calculation irrespective of the numbers involved. Procedural calculation is often associated with the use of standard written methods. Another consideration when defining mental arithmetic is whether it can still be considered mental if equipment such as number cards or number lines are used. While acknowledging that some of these activities can be seen as mental, I will deal with them in a separate chapter. Finally, although this chapter deals with mental arithmetic, mental mathematics is a wider category which, as Fielker (1997) reminds us, also includes other aspects of mathematics such as mental geometry.

Mental calculation and low attainers

The emphasis on mental calculation is likely to have mixed results for children regarded as low attainers in mathematics. For many, the implied reduction of written work can be an advantage. However, there is evidence to suggest that many children who experience difficulties with mathematics have particular problems in learning number facts (Denvir and Brown 1986). Some writers have paid particular attention to this, offering strategies to help children who have difficulties in retaining number facts (Chinn 1996). A study by Gray (1991) found that in addition to problems with remembering number facts, low attainers had a limited range of strategies to call on when working them out. An intervention study done by Askew *et al.* (1997) reported some success in encouraging low-attaining children to draw on a wider range of strategies. Examples of possible strategies for mental addition and subtraction are offered by Alam *et al.* (1994) in a book intended mainly for teachers of Year 3 and 4 children experiencing some difficulties in number.

In the classrooms

All four sets made frequent use of mental activities to start lessons, though there was a difference in the types of activity used and the length of time spent on them. Some examples of these 'mental starters' are given below. In the special needs set, mental starters often involved counting. In the other sets, activities related to multiplication facts, usually referred to as 'times tables', were more common. In all the sets a considerable amount of time was devoted to the recall of number facts, with a variety of approaches used, including games.

There was a difference between the sets in the role of mental calculation outside the mental starter. One teacher appeared to see mental arithmetic and teaching calculations as separate parts of the lesson, while one often taught mental methods of calculation in the main part of the lesson. The children also varied considerably in their preference for or against mental methods of calculation.

Mental starters

The first mental starter I saw in the original Year 5 set is described below:

The lesson started with a discussion of multiplication by 4. To start with, individual children were asked number facts, using terminology such as '3 times 4'. One child was asked to recite the '4 times table'. The teacher moved on to a discussion of other words for 'times'. He drew the multiplication symbol on the board, explaining to the children, 'It's not add and it's not a kiss.' He moved on to a discussion of commutativity. Next the children were given a worksheet about multiplying by 4.

The mental starter described above is typical of starters used in this set for many reasons. First, focusing on one multiplication table for a starter was very common, as was an attempt to approach it in many ways including discussion of language, symbols and properties of multiplication mixed with a little humour. This set also sometimes did worksheets as part of the mental starter as described above. The starter was followed by a main activity about subtraction of three-digit numbers. In this part of the lesson, formal written methods were used and there was no connection with the mental starter. Almost exactly two years after this lesson was observed, I spent my first lesson with the lower set. The first part of the lesson is described here:

Before the lesson started, the teacher had written the 4 times table on the board. The lesson started with the children reciting the table together fairly slowly. Next, they recited it at a much brisker pace. Finally, they were all asked to shut their eyes and recite it from memory. The next activity involved reading numbers displayed by the teacher.

In almost every lesson I saw in this set, the routine of reciting a table together, faster, then with eyes closed was used. The table used for this varied over the weeks. Sometimes the teacher spent time discussing the table and looking for number patterns within it. After the tables recitation, they moved on to other mental activities, sometimes in the form of games.

Counting

Counting activities were a very common part of the mental starter in the special needs set. The activities involved counting in ones, twos, fives and tens, both forwards and backwards. The teacher went to some trouble to vary the way this was presented. For example, the class counted together, children counted alone, they counted round in a circle. Sometimes they counted using pictures, sometimes they used coins or a hundred square. Counting was by no means error-free and some examples of this are given here:

> The children were sitting in a circle and counting round in fives, starting from 20. James had to follow 40 and said 60. Later, he had to follow 20. He said 105, then corrected it to 25.

> Neil was asked to count alone in fives to 100. He started slowly and deliberately. He started 5, 10, 15, 20, 13. Asked to try again, he said 20, 25, 30 and was then correct to 70. He was unsure whether 74 or 75 was next and was helped by the adults. He ended with 80, 85, 100.

> Michael was counting on his own in tens. He followed 90 with 20.

> Seth was counting alone in fives to 100. He was correct to 85 but followed this with 100. On his next attempt he said 85, 90, 99, 100.

Some of the above exemplify well-known difficulties. Numbers in the teens are known to cause problems when written but can also cause problems when spoken because they sound so much like the decade numbers. So, for example, Michael may have followed 90 with 20 because the sequence 70, 80, 90 sounded very similar to 17, 18, 19. Children are also known to have counting problems at boundaries such as 100. Sometimes when the children were asked to count to a particular number, they seemed to have a problem as they approached it, as shown by Neil and Seth in the examples above.

A possible clue to Neil's other problems lay in the speed at which he counted. The fact that he counted slowly but with apparent concentration suggests that he was possibly counting on five in ones in his head. This would account for the time taken and for the fact that he suggested 74 after 70. The fact that he was doubtful about this suggests he was beginning to see a pattern in the multiples of 5 but he was not able to use this to count in fives directly. It is harder to reach an explanation for James's difficulties, however; his responses raise an important point which was sometimes discussed among the adults. This was whether there was always a mathematical reason for children's incorrect answers or whether they sometimes did just say any number, either because they were just guessing or because they had lost concentration and missed the question. Although there was often much to be learnt from incorrect answers, there was a feeling that sometimes we could be looking for explanations that weren't there.

Recall of facts

In practice, recall of number facts usually meant work related to multiplication of single-digit numbers referred to by adults and children as 'times tables'. Work on times tables had a central place in mental starters for all but the special needs set. They concentrated on addition and subtraction rather than multiplication or division. However, this did not mean they did not work on the times tables. They worked on the 2, 5 and 10 times tables which were linked to counting in twos, fives and tens which were common activities in the classroom. They usually used a tables tape to which they would sing along. This was followed by individuals being given the opportunity to recite the appropriate table and have their name ticked off on a chart.

For all groups of children, it seemed that the learning of tables was a central activity with large amounts of time being spent on this. The teachers were inventive in their approaches using games, music and computer activities alongside tests and worksheets. The children were also encouraged to spend time learning their tables at home. The teachers helped by drawing their attention to number patterns and discussing properties of multiplication and reminding them about the symbol and associated language.

Given the enormous amount of time and energy invested in the learning of tables, an obvious question is whether the children retained this information. Sometimes it was impossible to say whether or not children knew their tables or even knew one particular tables fact. A good example of this is at the start of this chapter where Damian gets a question right but gets it wrong when it is repeated soon afterwards. Perhaps this could be seen as a negative maths fairy moment when knowledge mysteriously disappeared. Perhaps it was not so mysterious but relates to Damian being excited or under pressure. Such a moment could also be interpreted as confirmation that Damian did not really know his tables.

In general, children's apparent ability to remember tables facts seemed to depend on how tables knowledge was assessed. In practice, there was an element of assessment alongside the learning when children were asked questions verbally, asked to recite with their eyes shut or invited to recite alone. Tables were also assessed more directly and one example of this is given below. The example is drawn from a lesson with the later Year 5 set, early in the autumn term:

> The lesson started with a written test on the 5 times table. The questions were phrased slightly differently, sometimes using the word 'times', sometimes 'multiply', sometimes 'groups of'. There were ten questions and some were repeated, albeit using slightly different language. The questions asked once were 0×5, 1×5, 2×5, 5×5, 7×5 and 10×5. Questions asked twice were 3×5 and 4×5. The teacher did not ask 6×5, 8×5 or 9×5. At the end of the test, the answers were read out by the teacher and the children marked their own. On my table, Adrian and Bryn got 9 out of 10 and Nadeem and Matthew got 10 out of 10. Other groups in the class were equally successful.

The story above shows children's success at retaining tables facts. It also illustrates what appeared to be optimum conditions for this to happen. First, the questions all concerned one table. They had been working on this table since the start of term two weeks earlier and had been encouraged to learn it at home as well. The questions were asked in a fairly straightforward way. Although there was some variation in the language used, all the problems were about multiplying and all were expressed as straightforward calculations rather than in context. Two other factors which may have had a bearing on the results were the fact that the 5 times table chart was on the classroom wall throughout the test and that the children were allowed to mark their own work. My feeling at the time was that the boys I was sitting with had completed most or all of the questions genuinely.

The retention of tables facts seemed a lot more problematic when assessed in other ways. Children soon ran into difficulty if different tables were mixed, if multiplication was mixed with other operations or if calculations were presented in context. They also had difficulty in recalling multiplication facts in order to solve problems, especially when several steps were involved. Some examples of such situations are given below. These examples are chosen because they involve the same Year 5 set who seemed to know the 5 times table in the incident above:

During a lesson at the end of January, the children were completing a worksheet on multiplication of three-digit by one-digit numbers using vertical layout. I worked with Susan and Ella, who were struggling to remember the formal algorithm they had been taught. I noticed that they seemed to have difficulties with multiplications easier than those they got right in the tables test. For example, they did not answer 5×2. They also did not realise that the size of some of their answers was not sensible. For example, $7 \times 2 = 3$.

Towards the beginning of a lesson in March, the teacher was asking mental arithmetic questions and the children had to show the answers using number fans. I was sitting on a table with Nadeem, Lawrence, Susan and Ella. At one point, the children were asked to add on 5×20. All those on my table needed help with this. First we did 5×2, then 10×10. The children could not do either of these without assistance.

Games

Another way used to practise recall of number facts was in the form of games. These tended to include an element of competition, sometimes between individuals, sometimes between teams of children and sometimes between the children and the teacher. The teachers were all positive about the use of games, though in one set direct competition was rarely used. The children also displayed enthusiasm, often asking if they could play some of their favourite games. What is less clear is whether using the game format meant that the children were more likely to give correct answers. Sometimes this was far from the case. In the example below, the same Year 5 children described above working at the 5 times table were playing a team game.

One lesson in June, the mental arithmetic took the form of a game, carried out in teams. The teacher introduced this by referring to *Survivor*, a programme that had been on television the night before and involved teamwork. The game was called 'shuttle run whisper'. The game involved children carrying out calculations from the board and whispering answers to each other and eventually to an adult. At one point, the calculation on the board was 5 times 2 plus 20 subtract 12. I had mentally worked out the answer 18 and when Bob whispered the answer 27 to me, he could see from my face that he was wrong. The other team also failed to get the answer. The teacher attempted to find out what had gone wrong but this just added to the confusion. Lauren, who went first, claimed to have got the answer 37 but Anja misheard this as 27. Bryn also received the answer 27 but admitted he did not check because of the time limit. Bob said that he did check the answer of 27 and agreed with it.

The majority of calculations done in this session seemed to be answered incorrectly, like the example described here. This provided a contrast to written tests when children seemed more successful. I was unsure of the reason for this, though it could simply be that the calculation was harder. Another possibility is that the children did not seem to think it was so important to get spoken answers correct. A further possibility is that the game format, including a time limit, a competitive element and relatively complex rules, actually hindered the children's ability to calculate rather than providing the motivation that the teacher had hoped for.

The idea of a team game was also used by the teacher of the lower set, but in this case the whole class formed a team competing against the teacher. The game in question was called 'Pairs'. I first became aware of this game when I was helping in the classroom next door. The playing of Pairs caused so much excitement that we could tell next door that something was happening and the children explained that it was a game. I was therefore interested a few weeks later when I was in the classroom and a game of Pairs was announced:

The teacher drew a chart on the board with the headings 'Me' and 'Class'. It turned out that this was about how many points the teacher would need to get to win the game. A target of 25 was agreed. There seemed to be great excitement at the prospect of beating the teacher. One child told me in a whisper, 'We all get a sweet if we win', though later she admitted, 'He always wins.' The teacher had sixteen cards with numbers written on them, which paired to make 50. The cards were blue-tacked, face down, to the board. A child had to nominate two cards to be turned over, one after the other. If they totalled 50, the class got a point and the cards were removed from the game. If the cards did not total 50, the teacher got a point and the cards were turned back over. The children needed to find all eight pairs before the teacher reached 25 points. I was very surprised that they did not expect to win in this many turns. The children were desperate to have a turn but despite hoping to win as a team, they were not working together. When numbers did not total 50 they were simply replaced and the next person had another go. Many seemed to think they could do better than the others but few, if any, seemed to realise that this could be done by remembering where cards were. That does not mean that the mathematics was lost. Each time a card was turned over, the teacher and the class worked out together what should be added to it to make 50. They had considerable practice at doing this and this was in fact used in the main part of the lesson which was about finding pairs to 50 using an empty number line.

I did not see the children play Pairs again for quite a while, though they did play it on some days when I wasn't there. The next game of Pairs I saw was eight months after the first one:

> The cards for Pairs were already on the board before the lesson started and I think they had played the game the previous day. I noticed that one child had a quick look under a few of the cards on his way in. It was quite a while before the game was played so it's unlikely that he remembered where the numbers were. What is more significant is that he had realised that knowing where the numbers were would help them to win. This time a teacher target of 18 was agreed. In fact, the teacher only scored 10 points before the children had captured all eight pairs.

The Pairs incident illustrates some points which occurred with other games. The first time the children played, they were very excited about the format and the prospect of winning but not really informed about the game and possible winning strategies. It was only when the games had been played a few times that the children started to calculate more accurately and develop winning strategies. Usually games were rationed by the teachers and thus did not become so common that the children lost interest. There seemed to be a point where children were still enthusiastic about a game but able to concentrate on the mathematics rather than the format and were also familiar enough with what was required. There was one respect in which Pairs differed from most of the other games I saw and that was that within reason there was no time limit. Sometimes games depended on children answering before each other and I wondered if this sometimes encouraged children to guess rather than work the answer out. One example of this was the shoot-out game described at the start of this chapter. Occasionally children playing this game would give several incorrect answers in quick succession rather than taking time to work out the correct answer.

Mental calculation

In all the classes, there were occasions when the children carried out calculations mentally rather than merely trying to recall known facts. However, the teachers varied in how much emphasis they put on this. One teacher appeared to see mental arithmetic and teaching calculations as separate parts of the lesson. However, there were times when the children were expected to calculate mentally, most commonly during mental arithmetic tests. In the example below, Darren, one of the whisperers, made whispered comments suggesting he wanted to explain his answer. He repeated these comments in a louder voice and was eventually heard by the teacher:

> The teacher was reading out answers to a mental arithmetic test. Darren wanted to explain how he had done one of the questions (from 26, take away 11). The teacher seemed to ignore this for a while and continued to give answers. However, Darren persisted and was eventually allowed to explain how he had reached the answer. Darren said, 'Take away 1, 25 are left. Take away 10, leaves 15.' The teacher moved on to the next question. Darren's comment was not used or praised.

In this incident, the teacher does not seem to attach great importance to the method of mental calculation used. However, other teachers spent time discussing mental methods and sometimes taught specific methods. One example of this was in the special needs set where the teacher tried to explicitly teach children how to add using the count-on method. Generally, the children joined in with this method and were able to reach correct answers given some assistance. An exception to this was James, who did not always join in when the count-on method was specified:

> The children were sitting on the mat and were being asked to add numbers using the count-on method. For example, for 4 + 3 the teacher said, 'Put 4 in your head and count on 3.' The children held up three fingers and used them to count on, '... five, six, seven.' James was asked to join in, first by the teacher then by the support assistant who worked with him. Later in the same

lesson, I worked with James on a task involving similar calculations. He got the answers correct but arrived at them using cubes and the count-all method.

In the incident above, James initially did not participate in the task. This is discussed in more detail elsewhere (Houssart 2002a). Sometimes the adults did manage to get him to participate when the count-on method was used, though he always seemed reluctant.

The lower set teacher often taught methods of mental calculation or encouraged children to move from partly written methods to mental methods. One example of this was in calculating pairs of numbers to certain totals:

> The teacher told the children that they were going to work out some pairs to a hundred, reminding them that they had done this yesterday. He asked if they wanted help on the board and most did. The teacher wrote 100 on the board and, underneath, the symbols T and U. He reminded them that the tens should add to 9 and the units to 10. The first example was 63 and the children correctly provided 37. After several examples, the teacher said, 'Shall we raise the total a bit?' A total of 1,000 was agreed and the headings HTU written on the board. There was quite a lot of discussion about the totals needed in each column.

A week later, the children repeated the activity of finding pairs to 100. This time the activity was entirely mental with no prompts on the board.

Discussion

The place of mental arithmetic

Mental arithmetic seemed to have a different place in each set. In one set, for example, mental arithmetic was confined mainly to the first part of the lesson and mental methods were not encouraged elsewhere. The emphasis was on recall of facts rather than developing mental strategies. In another set, mental strategies were a more integral part of most mathematics lessons. The differences in mental work between the sets can be explained in various ways. The teachers seemed to have personal preferences for certain methods of calculation. To some extent, this was influenced by factors within the school such as the extent of training for the numeracy strategy together with the message in this training and the degree to which teachers were expected to comply with it.

Individual pupils also seemed to have preferences. Sometimes it seemed that pupil preferences did not match those of the teacher. Examples of this are Sean and Darren, who both displayed a preference for mental and strategic approaches, despite having a teacher who put more emphasis on procedural and written approaches. Sean also seemed able to vary his method according to the numbers involved. Thus he could do $112 - 100$ easily without recourse to a written method. Sean's approach to calculation is what Askew (2001) calls 'strategic'. In other words, the method of calculation is in part determined by the numbers involved. Darren showed a similar ability to alter his method according to the numbers involved as indicated by the incident after the mental arithmetic test.

There were other children in Sean and Darren's set who preferred a procedural approach and hence were more in line with the teacher. Julie is one example of this and her relative success with procedural methods will be discussed in another chapter. What is harder to ascertain is how many children in the set accepted the dominance of procedural methods because that is what the teacher offered. It is possible that there were children who may have coped better with an emphasis on mental methods but, unlike Sean and Darren, were not prepared to take a line contrary to that of their teacher.

In sets where the teachers showed a preference for mental methods, there were also some children who this did not suit. One example is Claire, whose preference for written work will be discussed in a later chapter. It seemed that whatever approach the teacher took, it was likely to help the majority of the children but not all of them. It was not a case of a 'correct' approach or one in line with the numeracy strategy. It was a case of different approaches suiting different children.

Multiplication facts

Despite the different styles and preferences of the teachers, they gave similar prominence to the learning of multiplication facts or times tables. This was true even for the set whose work on calculation dealt with addition and subtraction rather than multiplication. In all classes a large amount of time was devoted to the learning of tables facts. Teachers were also very inventive in varying their approach to this and using different strategies to help children. Despite this, children's difficulties in recalling facts persisted. They had some success when tables knowledge was assessed in a fairly limited way but experienced difficulties in other situations, especially when a fact had to be recalled as part of a more complex calculation. This raises the question of whether time spent on times tables is repaid by the children's performance.

Number games

Number games had a clear role as a motivating factor and were popular with children and teachers. However, closer observation suggests that some games were more successful than others in terms of children reaching correct answers. Sometimes when a game was first played children were preoccupied with the format or context. When games were repeated, the excitement subsided and children became more adept at developing winning strategies. In some cases, where a time limit was involved, this mitigated against calculation and encouraged children to guess. When this happened it was sometimes countered by the teacher skilfully adapting the rules so that those guessing were unlikely to be more successful than those calculating.

Classroom suggestions

Observing and listening

When children are engaged in counting activities, teachers and other adults in the classroom may take the opportunity to listen for difficulties experienced by individuals, or perhaps the group as a whole. My findings suggest they may hear evidence of the following:

- confusion between teen numbers and multiples of ten;
- problems in counting at tens and hundreds boundaries;
- problems as the end number in a count is approached;
- slow counting in tens or fives suggesting counting in ones is possibly being used.

As children work on calculations, adults may sometimes identify the following:

- strong preference for or against mental methods;
- enthusiasm for developing and explaining methods to suit particular numbers;
- strong resistance to particular methods of calculation.

Planning and teaching

When planning and teaching, use can be made of these observations to consider whether children should be encouraged to calculate in particular ways, or offered options. Teachers might also like to consider the following when calculations are carried out:

- asking if anyone carried out the calculation another way and offering them the opportunity to explain their method;
- explicitly discussing whether children prefer to do certain calculations mentally, in writing or with equipment and encouraging them to say why.

My observations suggest that games can be a popular context for mental calculation or recall of facts, but it cannot be assumed they automatically encourage the quick and accurate recall of facts. Teachers might wish to consider the following:

- *Familiarity of games*: Children are likely to be more successful at the mathematics when they have some familiarity with the rules of the game and possible winning strategies.
- *Frequency of games*: The first time a game is introduced children may be excited by the context at the expense of engaging with the mathematics. In contrast, if a game is played too often, it can lose its appeal.
- *Adapting rules*: Rules can be adapted to encourage children to work out answers to questions they don't know, rather than saying any number because of the time limit.

4 Number equipment

Number fans were given out at the beginning of a Year 5 lesson and as usual I was given the same as the children. I thought they looked new but Susan, who was sitting next to me, said they had used them the day before. She also added, 'But you're not allowed to muck about with them, Miss.'

Introduction

This chapter concerns number equipment which provides children with two-dimensional images; such equipment is sometimes referred to as 'representations'. It focuses on those types of representation which I saw used in the classrooms, namely hundred squares, number lines and various kinds of number cards. As the background reading section shows, representations were growing in popularity at the time of this study. They were also considered by some people to be particularly helpful for low attainers. This chapter concludes that this equipment helped some children, in particular, in reducing the need for recording and that it sometimes led to interesting comments from the children. However, for some children such equipment was not always helpful and was sometimes misunderstood.

Background

Changes in the use of number equipment

Until recently, there was a mixed picture in English schools as far as use of number representations was concerned. This is partly because use of base ten blocks, known as Dienes, dominated. As criticism grew of mathematics teaching in England, alongside comparison with other countries, one theme of the comparison was different use of number equipment. An example of this was a consideration of how hundred squares were used in Germany and Switzerland compared to their use in England (Bierhoff 1996). Bierhoff suggests that continental textbooks pay more attention to providing younger pupils with a complete overview of numbers in the range one to hundred, for example, by the use of visual aids such as hundred squares or number lines. She says use of hundred squares in England is often after the pupils have been introduced to numbers in this range. She goes on to say that hundred square use in English textbooks is often related to pattern and suggests that sometimes colouring in and colour patterns receive more emphasis than number patterns. Another important influence on use of number equipment has been work from the Netherlands on the use of number lines as reported by Anghileri (2001). She reports how use of practical equipment has declined in the Netherlands with more emphasis put on the number line and particularly the empty number line as a way of developing mental strategies.

Number equipment and the National Numeracy Strategy

The National Numeracy Strategy (DfEE 1999a) clearly encourages the use of certain resources, though it is acknowledged that there will be some variation according to the age of the children. The use of number lines of various types is clearly advocated, as is the use of number cards. Number cards might be digit cards, marked with single-digit numbers, place value cards which also contain multiples of ten and a hundred so that numbers can be built up, symbol cards or addition and subtraction cards for number bonds. The third piece of equipment strongly advocated is the hundred square with a large hundred square seen as essential in Years 2 to 4.

Justifications for equipment use

Those suggesting activities using equipment point to the fact that it provides pupils with an image of the number system. For example, Askew *et al.* (1996) use the category 'Lines cards and grids' as one of six sorts of experience they suggest children should be provided with. In justifying this, they explain that becoming confident with number involves having a sense of the magnitude of numbers and having a repertoire of symbolic images to draw upon. They go on to say that these materials provide rich sources of activity and offer children a range of mental images which can support the development of mental strategies.

The link between number equipment and mental calculation is made elsewhere. For example, a booklet on teaching mental calculation (QCA 1999a) includes activities using number lines, cards and grids. Sometimes particular pieces of equipment are associated with particular methods of calculation. For example, Merttens (1996) argues that use of number lines is crucial in helping children progress from counting to counting on. Talking particularly about younger children, she advocates the use of various types of line which consist of numbers as positions in a line. The empty number line is a variation suggested for older children. In the Netherlands, this is a frequently used model seen as a progression from earlier number lines such as those made from strings of beads, as explained by Van den Heuvel-Panhuizen (2001). An empty number line is simply a line on which only a few numbers are marked as required. For example, if children were using a number line to count on from 19 to 30, they might only need the numbers 19, 20 and 30 marked. Use of various empty number lines for calculations is described by Bramald (2000). For addition of two-digit numbers, Beishuizen (1993) argues that the use of a hundred square can encourage children to use strategies which involve adding tens, then units, to the starting number.

Another way of using number equipment is to enable children to give answers in oral sessions. This means that a teacher can ask a question of a whole class and the children can all show their answers by some means. Examples of 'answering devices' given by Harries and Spooner (2000) include digit cards.

Number equipment and low attainers

My own interviews with teachers support the view that teachers regard number equipment as more suitable for low attainers (Houssart 2001a). This view is in line with the national numeracy project which advocates frequent use of hundred squares and number apparatus in the section dealing with pupils with particular needs (DfEE 1999a). However, the association of number equipment and learning difficulties is not accepted by everyone. One critic of this approach is Seeger (1998) who uses the phrase 'representational overkill'. He suggests that this can have a devastating influence on those students it is supposed to help. He challenges the view that use of representations helps low-attaining students by making complex ideas seem simpler. He argues that instead, these students now have two problems: understanding the representations and understanding the numbers, and that they do not necessarily make connections between the two.

Advocates of using number equipment with low attainers do not necessarily only advise use of equipment, but rather suggest teaching approaches or structured programmes of which number equipment is but one part. One example of this is the work of Alam *et al.* (1994), who suggest activities aimed mainly at Year 3 and 4 children experiencing some difficulties with number. Many of the activities they suggest are based on number lines or hundred squares. Number cards are also used, as are other types of apparatus. An example drawn from the Netherlands is in the work of Menne (2001) who describes a research programme carried out with 200 low-attaining Year 3 children. An important part of this programme is the use of number lines and other representations.

In the classrooms

There was considerable variation in how much number equipment was used between the four sets. The special needs set were high users of equipment. Almost all their lessons included some use of equipment such as hundred squares, number lines or number cards. The equipment was evident in the classroom, both on the wall and on the children's tables.

The later Year 5 set were medium users of equipment, using it in about a third of all lessons. They used hundred squares most and used a counting stick once. Number fans, which are basically digit cards joined together in a fan form, were also occasionally used.

The other two sets were low users of equipment, both using it in only about one in six lessons. In the original Year 5 set hundred squares were used once for tables work, number fans were used once as answering devices and digit cards were used twice for place value activities. In the lower set, one lesson was based on the empty number line and one lesson made use of hundred squares. This set sometimes used number cards for games such as Pairs which was described in the last chapter.

Hundred squares

Hundred squares were frequently used by the special needs set. They took several forms. There was a large hundred square on the wall and two large squares with magnetic numbers. Children also sometimes used individual squares on card. Using the magnetic squares was a popular activity which children often chose to do at the beginning of a lesson. Some examples of this are given:

> Seth and Quam Nam chose to work on the magnetic hundred square. They were given the base and the multiples of five only. The task was to place them in their correct positions on the square. Quam Nam picked up a 5 and seemed to have difficulty in deciding where to put it. He started by putting it in a corner. I helped him to count across the base from 1 and the 5 was then placed correctly. Next, they tried to place the 10. To start with, they put it just after the 5 but realised fairly quickly they were wrong and moved it to the correct place. They picked up the 25 next and started by putting it immediately below the 5 but then moved it quite quickly. After this, they progressed much faster, making few mistakes. They counted down the columns and touched numbers with their fingers as they went.

This story suggests that positioning numbers on a hundred square was not a straightforward activity even for Seth and Quam Nam, who were both in Year 4 and had less difficulty with mathematics than most of the set. I observed Quam Nam working with a hundred square on other occasions and noticed that he became much more proficient at putting it together. Some children had much greater difficulty. An example of this is Neil whose work is described here:

> Early in the lesson, Neil chose to work alone on the magnetic number square. He placed seven numbers underneath each other in a column, but there seemed to be little or no pattern in either the numbers he selected or the order he put them in. The numbers, starting from the top, were, 79, 59, 31, 97, 42, 29, 69 (see Figure 4.1).

As with many incidents, this is open to more than one interpretation. Neil often seemed to experience considerable difficulties with understanding numbers and it could be that his response to the activity was a reflection of this. Another interpretation is that his difficulty was not necessarily with the number system itself but with the hundred square and he simply could not remember how it was put together. A third possibility is that Neil was not making a serious attempt to carry out the activity as envisaged by the teacher but was simply enjoying putting magnetic squares in a row on the board.

The teacher made use of the large hundred square on the wall for

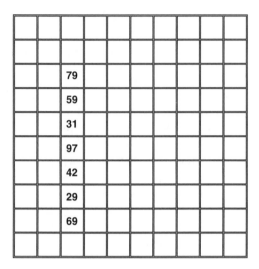

Figure 4.1 Neil arranges magnetic tiles on a hundred square

whole class activities when the children were sitting on the mat. Sometimes, it was used for counting, for example, in steps of ten or in twos. Some other activities using the large hundred square are described:

> Before the lesson, the teacher had prepared a sticker with each child's name on and had put them on top of numbers on the hundred square. Children were asked in turn to identify the number under their name and they were then asked questions about it. This caused considerable difficulty. Damian went first and correctly identified his number as 23. Asked for the number, 'ten more', he replied, '24' and asked for the number, 'one less', he said, '13'. Seth was next, his number was 88. The teacher asked for the number 'ten less' and he said, '87'. Asked for the number, 'one less', he replied first, '78', then, '87'. Michael was next and he knew that the number under his name was 26. Asked for the number, 'one less', he replied, '36'. The teacher helped him by asking him to imagine that he had 26 sweets and gave one away. Michael knew that he would then have 25 sweets. Next, the teacher asked him the number, 'one more'. She pointed to the square marked 27 but Michael read it as '72'. She asked him again the number one more than 26, and he said, '36'.

It is interesting to speculate why this activity caused the children such difficulty. Michael's response is especially revealing in that it shows that he understood the idea of one less in another context but not in the context of a hundred square. Most of the incorrect answers given suggested that children were looking at one of the squares bordering their square but usually not the correct one. It could be that they knew the answer was one of these four and simply guessed. The children's difficulties raised the question of the purpose of this activity. If it was to introduce them to the idea of more or less, it seemed likely that this would be done more successfully using the idea of sweets. What seems more likely, given subsequent activities, is that the teacher wanted them to understand more and less than on a hundred square in order to use it as a tool for addition and subtraction. The lesson just described took place in November. The following March, the children progressed to an activity which concentrated on finding numbers 10 or 20 more than a given number on the hundred square. In May, a lesson started with a similar activity to this but moved on to addition. The lesson used a large plastic spider which the teacher moved around the hundred square:

> The teacher started the lesson by talking to the children about the work they had done the day before using the spider and the hundred square. She reminded them that going along the row means counting in ones and going down means counting in tens. Then the spider was introduced and we worked on finding numbers 20 more and 10 more than the number the spider was on. Next, the teacher made the activity harder. The spider was on 38. She asked Quam Nam the number 20 more and he correctly replied, '58'. She then asked for the number 22 more than the spider and he correctly said, '60'. This was followed by more examples where children had to add first multiples of 10, then units, to the starting number.

The session described above was followed by individual work, where all the children had their own hundred squares and unifix cubes and were asked to add two-digit numbers to a starting number. In most cases they did this correctly, though the calculation $16 + 15$ caused problems because the children did not know where to count on after 30.

The most common use of hundred squares in all but the youngest class was in relation to multiplication tables. Usually, the hundred square was used for children to identify and colour in multiples of a particular number. The first time I saw this happen was in the first term, when I was sitting between Julie and Sean. This activity led to Sean whispering a prediction and a generalisation, as reported in Chapter 2. Julie had less success with the task.

> The children were asked to count back 6 from 36 and colour the next number. There was a general consensus that the answer was 30. Julie arrived at the agreed answer despite using the hundred square incorrectly. She moved across the square in the wrong direction, dotting each number (including the starting number) with her pencil and counting out loud, '1, 2, 3, 4, 5, 6' (see Figure 4.2).

I saw similar activities in the two other classes. There were a few children who, like Julie, did not seem to be helped by the hundred square. Julian, for example, had great difficulty in marking multiples of 4 on a hundred square, but when I talked to him, he seemed to know the multiples already, but was hampered by the physical task of colouring in. However, many children seemed to be helped by the hundred square and would often predict what was going to happen next. One example of this was an activity described here, where I was sitting next to Matthew:

> The first instruction was to colour 'the product of 1 and 6'. Next was the 'product of 2 and 6.' Matthew whispered to me, 'Next one's 18.' The teacher then asked them to colour 'The next multiple of 6.' All my table did this correctly. The activity carried on like this with multiples of 6 being coloured one at a time with the teacher varying the language used. By the time the teacher was on 48, Matthew was on 60. Later, the teacher said the next question would be a race between '... Mrs Houssart, Matthew and Lawrence'. The question was 'How many sixes in 72?' Matthew answered 12 more or less instantly. This contrasted with the difficulty he had seemed to have with similar questions.

21	22	23	24	25	26	27	28	29	30
31	32	33	24	35	36	37	38	39	40

Figure 4.2 Julie counts back 6 from 36 on a hundred square

Matthew did seem to be helped by the hundred square and motivated to use it. It is possible, however, that his performance on the last question was due to the challenge of racing against an adult rather than the presence of the hundred square. Nevertheless, it was another maths fairy moment which reminded me that children sometimes perform much better on particular tasks than logical consideration of their attainment would lead us to believe.

Number lines

The special needs set used number lines marked with the numbers 1 to 20 in four lessons. In this set, I also saw a number line marked on the blackboard, a counting stick, a plastic number line used with felt-tip pens and a number line as part of a worksheet. Number lines were rarely used in other sets, though they were attached to the tables in one of the Year 5 sets.

In the special needs set, when number lines were used, this was often a suggested way of carrying out the calculations as part of an activity. Sometimes, all the children were given numberlines with the suggestion that they use them if they needed to. Sometimes they were available for those who wanted them:

> The children were working on an activity called Number Walls, which involved addition to 20. The children could use cubes or number lines to help with the addition. I was working with James, who preferred to use cubes. Later, Claire came to me with her work. She had chosen to use number lines and was able to do this but sometimes needed reminding to count 'one' on the first jump rather than the starting number. Seth seemed able to reach the correct answers without using either cubes or a number line.

This incident illustrates three possible responses to number lines. James preferred other aids to calculation, Claire seemed to be helped by a number line and Seth did not need any kind of aid. Another response I noticed from children, for example Joe, on other occasions was to use the number line for some calculations, working without it for a few, usually easier, ones.

The teacher of the lower set made use of empty number lines, drawn on the board, to assist children with calculations. The session described here followed the playing of the game Pairs described in the last chapter, which had involved finding pairs of numbers which total 50. The children had also used empty number lines to help them calculate the day before. The lesson started with the teacher reminding them of this before introducing a slightly different method. The new method involved jumping back to a multiple of 10, then jumping forward to 50:

The teacher wrote on the board:

$21 + \square = 50$

He then drew a number line where he went back 1 then forward 30. Underneath he wrote $30 - 1 = 29$ (see Figure 4.3).

The children were expected to carry out similar calculations using this method. The teacher explained how he wanted them to do this. He told them to draw the number line and the 'bumps' first. Underneath they were to write the big number first, take away the small one and fill in the answer.

Some of the children used pads for jottings. When I went to see how Damian was getting on, the jottings on his pad confirmed his difficulties. I explained again and drew the correct diagram on his pad, which he later copied and used to help him.

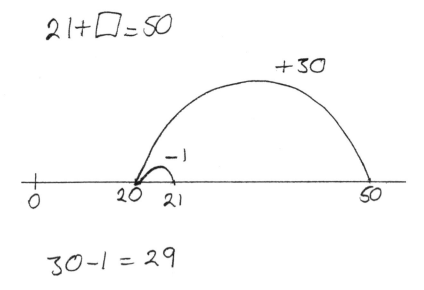

Figure 4.3 Whiteboard from number line lesson

Many of the children seemed to find this activity difficult and the teacher had to stop the class and explain it again. In the case of Damian, his jottings give some clue to his difficulties (see Figure 4.4). His first jotting may have been just a doodle (certainly he had a tendency to doodle) or may have been his view of what a number line looked like. His second diagram was drawn after more explanation had been given and has a similar appearance to those drawn by the teacher. Damian was working on the question $32 + \square = 50$. He did not identify 30 as the number to jump back to and many others in his group shared this difficulty. He put the number 20 on the number line instead. However, he incorrectly placed the 20 between the 32 and 50. Damian's response suggests that he did not understand what an empty number line is or how it might help with the question. In this case, it appeared that something designed to assist the children presented an additional problem to some of them.

Number cards

All four sets made some use of number cards. Cards of some type were used in about half of the lessons with the special needs set. These included digit cards, place value cards, larger cards with two-digit numbers on and cards made to look like front doors with numbers on. Cards were used for sequencing, especially counting in fives, twos and tens. They were also used for place value activities

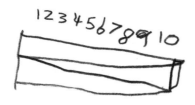

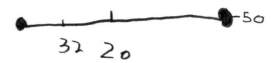

Figure 4.4 Damian's jottings from number line lesson

and as answering devices. Sometimes number cards were also used to generate and answer calculations. For example, children were asked to find two cards with a total of 10 or 20 or to find the difference between two cards. Number cards of some form were also used by all the other classes, with games and place value activities being common uses. Two of the sets used number fans as answering devices. This can be seen as a variation of number cards, as they are basically digit cards joined together.

Sequencing using the front door cards was often used as an optional activity at the start of lessons. I noticed that Ben often chose this activity. In the incident here, he was returning to an activity that he had done with help on previous weeks:

> At the start of the lesson, Ben worked alone putting the doors in order. He was quite slow and chose to put them in pairs beside each other. He started with 5, followed by 10. Underneath, he put 15 and 20 and underneath them he put 25 and 30. He completed the activity correctly but slowly. I encouraged him to read the numbers and say what he was looking for next.

Digit cards were sometimes used for children to make numbers. This was often connected with work on place value. In one lesson with the original Year 5 set, the children were given two of each digit and asked to make various numbers with them. Sometimes the teacher wrote sequences of numbers on the board and asked the children to make the next number using their cards:

> The children were asked to make an odd number between 316 and 320. Some of the children needed help with this. When the answer 317 was suggested, the teacher asked why it was odd. Sean whispered, 'Because you can't divide 7 by 2 people.'

> A little later, a sequence was formed by adding 2 to 317. It was agreed that 319 came next. Pedro volunteered the next answer 321, then added 323, in a whisper. Sean said in a whisper, 'It's easy. It's 2 more.'

> Later in the lesson, the activity changed to the children being asked to use 3 specified digits to make the largest possible number. At this point Sean stood up, went to the teacher and said, 'All you've gotta do . . .'

All the incidents above include comments made by the whisperers. They show that the children were commenting on the mathematics, including giving reasons and making generalisations. Such comments were common in activities like this but rarer during activities such as completion of worksheets. It is possible that not having to worry about recording left these children free to think and talk about what was happening to the numbers. In the activities above, place value activities were carried out using digit cards. With the Year 3 and 4 class, place value activities tended to make use of place value cards:

> It was the first time the children had used place value cards. They were asked to set them out in order with tens and units separately. I was sitting next to James, who managed the ordering reasonably, though he started with 30 after 10 but sorted this out. To start with, he looked for 11 to follow 10 and 100 to follow 90. The first task was to make 12. Claire had problems with this and other children had problems with 14, which followed. James answered the questions very well, needing no help with deciding which cards to pick up. He was slow but meticulous in putting the used cards back in the right place and the right way up.

Number fans, which can be seen as a variation on number cards, were used as answering devices by two of the classes. The first time I saw this happen with Year 5 children was the incident described at the beginning of the chapter. Fans were also used by the younger children, as described in the incident that follows. The session the incident is drawn from started with children being asked to show various numbers with their number fans. I noticed that James seemed to have physical difficulty in manipulating the fan. Douglas had to be reminded not to use his as a fan. Some children, such as Michael, reversed the digits of some of the numbers. After this, the teacher moved on to the main activity, which was about pairs of numbers which added to make 20. This was initially difficult and the teacher explained several times. The other adults in the room also helped individuals:

> The teacher moved on to the next example. She held up the card with the number 14 on it. The children had to work out what had to be added to it to make 20. She prompted the children by saying, 'What do you put with 4 to make 10?' 'I get it,' Neil shouted suddenly, getting very excited. Looking at his number

fan, he said, 'Mister Sixy, where are you?' In case anyone was in any doubt, this was followed by the comment, 'I know, I know.'

This incident seemed significant for Neil, in that he suddenly seemed to realise what was going on. Again, it is difficult to say whether the equipment being used played any part in this, but as before it did mean that the children were unhampered by the need to record answers.

Discussion

Did number equipment help?

The incidents in this chapter suggest a mixed picture as far as the use of number equipment is concerned. There were occasions when the equipment did seem to assist the children in reaching answers to calculations. It is more difficult to assess whether the equipment helped children in their understanding of the number system. Certainly when activities such as putting together the magnetic hundred square were frequently used, the children became more proficient at them. What is harder to say is whether they were learning about the number system or simply about the physical task of assembling that particular square.

Another way in which equipment might be seen to be helping is that it enabled children to carry out calculations without having to record the answers. This meant that it was likely that more examples could be covered in the time available and it also reduced the worries connected with written work, which will be discussed in Chapter 6. Number equipment particularly helped the whisperers, with activities based on equipment often resulting in them making remarks which included generalisations and comments about what they had noticed. Some other children also responded to equipment in this way.

My observation is that number equipment often helped but this depended on two main factors: frequency of use and preferences of individual children.

Frequency of use

The lesson with the empty number line illustrates how difficult it can be for some children when they are first asked to use a piece of number equipment in a particular way. Although this class had used empty number lines the day before, they were used in a different way. They had not had the experience of a gradual introduction to empty number lines, common in the Netherlands, as described by Bramald (2000) or the sort of structured programme described by Menne (2001). This lesson supports the view of Seeger (1998), who suggests that children can be faced with the dual task, in this case: both understanding the empty number line and working out the problems given. In other cases, such as the use of the hundred square for addition, familiarity with the equipment had been built up over the year and activities had been carried out as a preliminary to the addition itself. However, it should be remembered that the move from introducing the hundred square to using it to add on two-digit numbers took most of the school year.

Individual differences

In some of the incidents described, the number equipment suited some children better than others. It seemed to suit the whisperers as it reduced the need for formal recording and gave them opportunities to notice what was happening and predict what might happen next. The same activities did not seem to suit Julie. She did not seem to understand how to count back on a hundred square, but instead used the alternative strategy of seeing what answer the rest of the group gave.

For some children, some pieces of equipment worked better than others. A good example of this is James, who seemed to be assisted by place value cards and persevered with them despite slight physical difficulties. On the other hand, he avoided using number lines if possible. This could be linked to his difficulty in using the count-on method for addition as described in the previous chapter. As Merttens (1996) points out, the number line can be a way of encouraging children to progress to the count-on method. So encouraging James to use it could be seen as a way of helping him overcome this difficulty. However, this was not the case.

Children's choices

When given a choice of equipment, James was consistent in avoiding number lines but making use of other equipment. It seemed that the number line model did not help him. It is useful to relate his experience to the advice of Askew *et al.* (1996), who advocate that children should be given a range of mental images to draw on. In the case of James, providing this range enabled him to pick the model that seemed to help him.

Sometimes the children were only given one piece of equipment but had the option of whether to use it or not. On the occasions when I saw this happen, children made sensible choices. For example, Seth was aware that he could carry out the calculations without a number line. He did not use one. Joe, on the other hand, showed an awareness of those calculations he could do unaided, calling on the number line for others.

Classroom suggestions

Observing and listening

As the incidents above suggest, there can be considerable individual variation in how children respond to number equipment. The questions here may help adults working alongside children to discover some of these differences:

- Do the children know which direction to move when counting on using a hundred square?
- Do they know how to count on when they get to the end of a row?
- Can they use the square to count on or back in tens?
- When children add using a traditional number line, do they start at the first number or at zero?
- Do children counting on with the number line realise that they are counting the steps and should not count 'one' at the starting point?
- Do children using place value cards have difficulties with numbers in the teens?

The suggestions above relate to potential difficulties, but it is also worth listening for signs that children are reacting positively to activities based on number equipment. Ask yourself:

- Do children working with a hundred square indicate that they have noticed a pattern, either by commenting or by suddenly racing ahead with the activity?
- Can children continue sequencing activities further than planned by the teacher?
- Can children explain the pattern or the rule in sequencing activities?

- Can children make general statements about the numbers formed by digit cards?

Planning and teaching

My observations suggest that responses to use of number equipment will vary between children. The following are worth considering:

- Children may need to use a piece of equipment several times in order to be familiar enough with it for it to help.
- Some children may prefer particular pieces of equipment, so being presented with more than one model will help them.
- It is worth considering how often children have the opportunity to make choices about when to use equipment.
- Children who notice short cuts and patterns should be given opportunities to explain them.
- Some children may be able to extend ideas and activities.

5 Practical work

Each child was given a large pile of plastic money. Sean announced with a smile, 'I'm rich.' This was followed by an estimate of how much money was in the pile and a discussion of what it might buy, closely followed by speculation about how much money he might be given on his birthday.

Introduction

Practical work has, for a long time, been seen as a 'good thing' in English primary schools. As the background reading section to this chapter shows, this view was being questioned slightly at the time this study was carried out. The classroom section of this chapter illustrates the range of practical equipment I saw in use and the way the children responded to it. In common with the representations discussed in the last chapter, practical equipment did not always help all the children. Nevertheless, it often had a positive effect on the mathematical content of lessons. In particular, such lessons sometimes included more challenging aspects of number than were met in ordinary number lessons. Practical lessons also sometimes offered opportunities for problem-solving and decision-making. These things did not happen automatically and the role of adults was crucial.

Background

Practical work in primary mathematics

For many years there has been a view in English primary schools that practical work has an important place. This can be seen in teachers' guides such as the Nuffield guide with the slogan 'I do and I understand' and its emphasis on active learning (Nuffield Mathematics

Project 1967). Nuffield Mathematics is said by Thompson (1997) to have been a strong influence on most written primary mathematics resources for several decades. Practical activities are also strongly advocated in books written at about this time aimed at new or intending teachers (e.g. Williams and Shuard 1970). Since then, official documents have been seen as endorsing the importance of practical work. For example, the Cockroft Report includes 'appropriate practical work' in the list of six elements which should be included in mathematics teaching at all levels (Cockcroft 1982: paragraph 243). The section dealing with mathematics in the primary years goes further in suggesting that practical work is essential throughout the primary years. When the National Curriculum was introduced (DES 1989), research suggested that the section on 'Using and Applying Mathematics' was seen by many teachers as a call for practical work (SCAA 1993).

Justification for practical work

The place of practical work in learning mathematics is often supported by reference to the work of developmental psychologists. Probably the most influential of these is Piaget. His work had a strong influence on the Nuffield Project team, who dedicated their first publication to him (Nuffield Mathematics Project 1967). Piaget's work is also referred to in books which discuss how children learn mathematics. For example, Liebeck (1984) discusses the theories of various psychologists talking in detail about Piaget, but also discussing the work of others. Liebeck's own view is that young children learning mathematics should start with experience with physical objects. Wood (1988) provides another comparison of theories of learning. In discussing the work of Piaget and Bruner, he points out that, despite their differences, they share the view that action is the starting place for the action of symbolic thinking.

It is also important to consider what justification teachers themselves use for the inclusion of practical work. Moyer (2001) says that despite the large amount of research on practical equipment, which she refers to as manipulatives, observations and interviews of teachers using manipulatives in typical classrooms for their own purposes are lacking in the literature. She goes on to report a study carried out with middle-grade mathematics teachers in America. She found that teachers often saw use of manipulatives as 'fun' and to be used as a reward for good behaviour or for a 'nice break'. My own interviews with teachers about tasks they had used with their classes suggested an enthusiasm for practical tasks. This was even more marked among teachers of lower sets (Houssart 1999).

Practical work and non-number

How much practical work is included in teaching and learning mathematics is likely to expand with the breadth of mathematics being taught. When discussing changes in the English Mathematics curriculum between the 1960s and the 1980s, Brown (2001) talks of a broader mathematics curriculum in contrast to the previous emphasis on arithmetic. Thus, the period when practical work was popular was also a period when more time was likely to be spent on aspects of mathematics such as measuring and shape which easily lend themselves to practical work. Writing ten years before this study, Ainley (1991) describes a measurement lesson full of activity. She goes on to say that in primary schools, measurement formed a sizeable part of the mathematics curriculum. She continues by discussing the mathematics involved in measurement.

Structural apparatus

The use of structural apparatus in the teaching of number is discussed in more detail by Williams and Shuard (1970) who say that almost all types of structural number apparatus work on the principle of using length to represent number. One example is unifix cubes, individual plastic cubes, which can be joined together to make rods. A variation on this is the Dienes base ten apparatus. This consists of small wooden cubes which represent units, rods to represents tens, flats (equivalent to ten rods) to represent hundreds and cubes (equivalent to ten flats) to represent thousands. Anghileri (2001) says that traditionally children in English classrooms have used cubes such as unifix for early work on place value, followed by Dienes base ten apparatus for more advanced calculating. She points out the link between base ten apparatus and particular calculating procedures such as decomposition. There has been criticism of base ten apparatus. For example, Hart (1989) reports on research concerning use of base ten apparatus for subtraction. Her interviews with children showed that many disliked using the blocks and those that used them did not necessarily do so in a way that matched the formal algorithm.

Practical work in the National Numeracy Strategy

As has already been mentioned, mental calculation is stated as a central part of the Strategy and practical work has a much lower profile. The section about resources (DfEE 1999a) starts by talking in detail about the sort of number equipment discussed in the last chapter, such as number lines, cards and hundred squares. Following this, brief mention is made of other equipment children might use. The suggestions include small apparatus such as counters, cubes, dice and dominoes and measuring equipment, sets of shapes and construction kits. Later on it says that base ten apparatus can be used to show the relative size of units, tens, hundreds and thousands and for partitioning numbers. Teachers are advised that they should always use digit cards alongside the pieces. It seems that equipment is more likely to be used for aspects of mathematics other than number. However, the detail of the document suggests these aspects of mathematics may be less practical than might be imagined. It should also be remembered that the Strategy is dominated by number.

In the classrooms

There was variation between the sets in their use of practical equipment. One could be seen as high users, two were medium users and one was a low user. It is interesting to compare this with the use of number representations considered in the last chapter. The set making highest use of practical equipment were also the highest users of number representations. Similarly, the set making the least use of practical equipment was one of the low users of number representations.

The special needs set were the highest users of practical equipment, using it in 15 out of 25 lessons. They made regular use of cubes, dice, coins and money. In the two Year 5 sets, practical work featured in about half the lessons. This was often for lessons on measuring or shape, though practical work was sometimes included in number lessons, usually when a new idea was being introduced. The lowest users of practical equipment were the lower set, who used it in 8 out of 30 lessons. Two of these lessons dealt with shape, one with data handling and the others with aspects of measuring.

Practical number activities

The most frequently used equipment for teaching number was unifix cubes. These were occasionally used in one class to show tens and units, though this was less common than use of place value cards. It was more usual to see cubes used to model numerical operations. This often happened when an aspect of number was being introduced. The expectation seemed to be that this would serve as a good introduction that children would understand and later they would progress to working without the equipment. One example of this occurred in a Year 5 lesson about division by 3:

> Two girls were asked to give out 30 unifix cubes to each pair of children. This was a slow process, even though all three adults in the room helped at some point. This was because the children were both slow and inaccurate at counting out 30 cubes. The proposed sharing of cubes also presented a problem, with Bryn in particular being possessive about his cubes and refusing to share them with Matthew. Later the activity was adapted to be done alone and each child had 30 cubes. The children were asked to put their 30 cubes in a row and then to put them in groups of 3. All the children near me managed to do this, though some had a little help.

This purely practical activity was followed by use of a worksheet about division by 3 which the children completed using the cubes. At the end of the lesson, the teacher moved on to asking questions about division by 3 which he expected the children to answer without the cubes. This lesson seemed to help the children I was working with. For example, Nadeem needed help in the initial stages of grouping the cubes but then continued alone. He needed a little more help when he moved on to the worksheet but then completed it successfully. At the end of the lesson, he was able to answer questions about division by 3. This was true of others on my table, though not of everyone in the room. For example, the teacher directed one question at Stacey, one of the children in the class who had the greatest difficulty with mathematics. He asked her, 'How many groups of three in six?' He held up six fingers to help her and she replied, 'Fourteen.'

Cubes, fingers and small objects were also used for modelling addition and subtraction. The teacher of the special needs set also used large dominoes to introduce the idea of addition by finding the total number of spots on each domino.

> The teacher introduced a set of large wooden dominoes and told the children they were going to use them for a game. She started

with the domino that had six spots on one side and five on the other. The task was to find the total number of spots. This proved quite difficult and at one point the children were barely responding. The next example was 3 + 3 and the teacher encouraged the children to '. . . shoot your hands up really quickly'. James did as he was asked but unfortunately he had not worked out the answer. The next example was 1 + 1. This question was targeted at Claire, but despite encouragement from the classroom assistant near her, she did not give an answer.

The adults were surprised how difficult the children seemed to find this activity. The original plan had been to move on from the practical activity to a related worksheet. However, the teacher decided with the agreement of the other adults to leave the sheet and carry on with the practical and oral work. This prompted Claire to comment, 'Are we doing games all day?' The adult response to this was to talk about the importance of the *work* they were doing. It seems that Claire may not have regarded activities like this as work. The assumption at the time was that she did not answer the question about the domino because she could not do 1 + 1. As the year progressed, her relative success on written activities made us wonder whether she was giving practical work her full effort.

Money

One Year 5 lesson about money was almost entirely practical. The main activity during this lesson consisted of each child being given a large pile of plastic money to count. During this activity, I was sitting between Sean and Julie. There was a big difference in their response to the task, with Julie having considerable difficulty:

After initial hesitation Julie moved to sorting the coins by type, but counting them proved difficult for her. I suggested that we start with the larger amounts. She counted the pound coins without difficulty. Counting other coins proved harder. With prompting she was able to join me in counting the 10p coins in tens. When it came to the 2p coins, however, she rejected my suggestion that she might count them in twos. Instead she counted in ones, touching each coin twice. When it came to mixed amounts life got harder. For example, having established that the 50p and 20p she had totalled was 70p, Julie tried to add on some 10p coins. I tried addition, but she could not tell me what 70p + 10p was. My next suggestion was counting on in tens from 70. Although Julie could count in tens, she had to start at 10 each time, so she needed help with this method. When left to herself, I noticed she did 90 + 10 by counting on in ones using her fingers.

Sean seemed more at home in handling money, as can be seen from his comments reported at the start of this chapter.

Later in the lesson, the teacher asked children to convert numbers of certain coins to amounts of money. Sean was able to answer some of the harder questions arising from this. For example, he said how much 14 × 20p coins were worth, a question which stumped many of the others. He found the value of 33 × 50p coins and explained his method, which was based on working out the value of 10 × 50p coins, then 20 ×, then 30 ×, then 32 ×, then 33 ×.

In other classes, there were children who had considerable difficulty with money. An example is James:

I was working near James on a money task towards the end of the year. The children were given food packets with prices on and had to use cardboard coins to make the correct amount of money. James picked an item priced at 30p and had problems, so I suggested he swap it for one marked 6p. He laid out six 1p coins. I told him this was right and asked if it could be done any other way. He agreed it could be done with 2p coins, then laid out six 2p coins. I asked him to count them and he counted them as ones. I pointed out that they were twos and we counted together in twos. Later, he had to make 15p and laid out one 1p coin and one 5p coin next to each other (see Figure 5.1).

The difficulty James had counting 2p coins was probably because he was still treating the coins in the same way as he would treat cubes, with each representing one. Later on, he may have been confusing coins for large amounts with the sticks of cubes that had been used to explain tens and units to him. However, it is interesting to note that James's teacher only made occasional use of cubes in sticks of ten. Place value cards, which used 10 rather than 1 to represent ten, were used more frequently. Unfortunately, James did not seem to make the link between the card for 10 and the 10p coin.

Figure 5.1 James lays out coins to pay for an item costing 15p

Measuring

Most of the lessons on measuring were practical to some extent. For measuring length, children used rulers, metre sticks and pieces of string. The string proved problematic for some. The story here is drawn from the original Year 5 set:

> The teacher was introducing the idea of converting metres to centimetres, though a previous session had involved converting centimetres to millimetres. When the teacher said that one metre is a hundred centimetres, Sean whispered, 'A hundred centimetres is a thousand millimetres.' The teacher moved on to talking about a piece of string which he said was just under a metre long. Sean said in a whisper, 'Nine hundred and ninety-nine millimetres, perhaps.'

In the same lesson, the children used string to measure curves. I was sitting next to Julie, who needed help with this activity:

> Julie had to measure a piece of string which was longer than her 30 centimetre ruler. I tried to encourage her to suggest a way of measuring it, but without success. We established together that part of it was 30 centimetres long and we marked where that piece ended and placed the mark against the zero of the ruler. The rest of the string was 7 centimetres long, but knowing this did not seem to help Julie. I pointed out that the mark was at 30 centimetres and suggested we count on from there. I started counting at 31 and moving along 1 centimetre as I said each number. Julie slowly joined in and we arrived at an answer of 37.

The other Year 5 set also carried out measuring activities. The first lesson I saw dealt with measuring using non-standard units:

> The teacher was talking about the length of a table. He was holding up a toy motorbike and asked the children to estimate the length of the table in motorbikes. The children moved on to carrying out a similar activity themselves. Some of them were slightly side-tracked by the provision of toy cars for non-standard units. Lawrence found a lorry with a ladder attached and spent a lot of time on this. I worked with Matthew, who used my finger as a mark for where the toy car ended. My initial feeling was that he did not really understand how to measure using objects, as the marking and the moving of objects seemed to be a bit haphazard. However, I slowly realised that his many inaccuracies were moving his answers much nearer to the estimates that he had written before we started measuring.
>
> Some of the children were using large collections of objects for measuring, meaning that they could simply lay the objects in a line rather than having to worry about moving and marking. Even this strategy had its limitations when long measurements were required. At one point, the teacher stopped the class to discuss this. There was a line of 63 nails on the classroom floor as two children attempted to measure the length of the classroom in nails. The teacher had stopped the activity when the nails had reached the middle of the room. He asked the children measuring how many nails they had used and asked the class how many they thought would be needed to go all across the room. Lauren said, 'Double it.' She then got the correct answer of 126. Matthew, who was sitting next to me, whispered the incorrect answer of 213.

The calculation that Lauren had carried out in her head was harder than those the class had been working on and as far as I know she had not been taught a formal way of doing this. This was one of several examples where the number work involved in measuring lessons was more complex than that carried out in number lessons. Matthew did not obtain a correct answer to this particular calculation. This was a reminder to me that, like many children I listened to, he sometimes seemed to be in advance of what was being taught, but not always. Two weeks later, the same class were measuring in centimetres and the teacher was talking about centimetres and metres with a particular emphasis on how many centimetres in a metre:

The teacher started giving out metre sticks to pairs of children. He stipulated who should work with whom and also spent time pointing out the differences between the different types of metre stick. Christopher was asked to share a metre stick with Natalie. He refused to do so and was eventually sent out. The teacher then continued with his questions. He asked Malcolm how many centimetres there were in half a metre. He added that if he answered correctly he could use a metre stick on his own. Malcolm correctly answered 50.

A bit later, scissors and string were handed out. The children were asked to cut an estimated 20 centimetres from the string. On my table, I noticed that Nadeem and Adrian estimated as requested but Bryn and Matthew actually measured before cutting.

The lower set sometimes carried out measuring activities in connection with the perimeter of shapes:

The teacher had explained how to find the perimeter of shapes. He also reminded the children how to use rulers, including the fact that they should use the side of the ruler marked in centimetres and they should make sure they started at zero. He then gave out a sheet containing five rectangles, in all of which the sides were whole numbers of centimetres. The task was to measure the sides and calculate the perimeter for each shape. Damian seemed to be making good progress on this activity. He did the first two correctly without help, though he did make some jottings to assist him. When I went to see how he was getting on, he had just made a mistake in measuring the third shape. This was a thin rectangle, 11 centimetres high and 1 centimetre wide. He had recorded the width as 2 centimetres. I suggested that he measured this again. The teacher also joined us at this point and watched. Damian had the ruler upside down.

This incident illustrates a common occurrence, that of occasional mistakes. Damian appeared to be struggling with the third example, having an incorrect answer and then holding the ruler upside down. It was easy to conclude from this that he could not measure but actually I had watched from a distance as he had carried out earlier measurements and calculations correctly and without assistance.

Shape

Lessons on shape often used standard sets of plastic shapes. In the case of lessons about 2D shape, they were often used for drawing round:

> There was a large pile of assorted shapes on the centre of each table. The children were told to take about ten different shapes, draw around each one, cut it out and fold it to show the lines of symmetry. One immediate problem on my table was deciding what counted as a different shape. The collection on our table contained several regular polygons of similar size. There was a tendency for children to assume that these were all the same. This improved when the teacher stopped the activity and introduced the names of some of the shapes and talked about the number of sides.
>
> Later in the lesson, the teacher encouraged the children to move towards finding as many axes of symmetry as they could on each shape. Children responded differently to this. Linda seemed to find it really hard to find more than one axis on a shape and was inclined to give up. Erica started to realise that shapes had more than one axis and was able to mark them correctly. Sean showed particular interest in the circle. At one point he whispered, '. . . it can go anywhere through the middle, any line on the circle.' A similar comment was made by Darren, who said the circle could be folded '. . . in any way'. Although these comments were initially whispered, the children repeated them and the teacher heard them. He picked up on these comments and invited the children to share them with the rest of the class.

This incident suggests that shapes which were available to the children had an impact on the activity. They were using a mixture of several sets of shapes borrowed from different classrooms. This had an interesting consequence in that when the children were asked to find ten different shapes, they had to think carefully about what this meant. This actually introduced a fundamental mathematical idea. Also relevant to the children's response during the lesson was the range of shapes in the collection. In this case, the circle caused particular interest to some children while the large number of regular polygons with different numbers of sides proved challenging when it came to seeing different shapes.

Data handling

Data-handling lessons were very rare but when they did occur, they tended to be practical. The example that follows is drawn from the special needs set:

> The teacher produced a bag full of tubes of Smarties and asked the children about them. James said that they were different colours. The children also wanted to talk about whether they could eat the Smarties. They had worked on graphs the day before and Neil came up with the suggestion of making a graph to show the different colours in a tube of Smarties. Neil was called to the board and with the help of one of the classroom assistants managed to draw the axes and number the vertical axis. The adults suggested abbreviations for the colours and these were written on the board. Claire came to the board to write the letters. The children then went to their places to empty their Smartie tubes and draw their graphs. I was working next to Michael. I noticed that when he had eight Smarties in a line he miscounted them, making it seven. When he had to count all the Smarties at the end, he made several mistakes. He also had difficulty with the numbers on the graph, numbering the first square in each block as zero.

Like the measuring lessons described earlier, this lesson also provided opportunities to use number. In this case, the children had to utilise basic ideas such as counting objects and writing numbers. For Michael this proved useful practice and seemed an effective way of incorporating this in to ongoing work.

The lower set also had a data-handling lesson which had a practical element:

> The main activity for the lesson was to prepare a tally chart, then throw a dice 30 times and record the results. The results then had to be transferred to a bar chart. The teacher showed them how to do the tally chart and to start the graph. He also reminded them that they would need to keep track of how many throws they had done. He suggested this might be done by keeping a separate tally but did not go in to any more detail. Initially, the teacher and I held back while the children tried to organise the tally charts. Eventually we started to help those having difficulties. Julian did particularly well in this lesson. He worked without help and completed the task correctly. I was called over to help some of those

who rarely seemed to have difficulties. They all had problems because they had not kept count of their throws. When I returned to the group I usually helped, I noticed they seemed to be doing well. When I talked to the teacher, he said that he felt the 'slow' workers were completing this task before those who usually finished early. It seemed that the traditional 'fast' workers had simply thrown the dice lots of times without keeping count until they realised they had gone too far.

Some of the children had organised their work so that they threw the dice the correct number of times. The others had to take action to remedy this. For example, some of them carried out several mental additions in order to see whether their total was 30. Some also went on to work out how many more throws were needed.

Discussion

Starting with practical work

The main use of practical work related to number was in the introduction of new ideas. This meant that the children had a concrete model for what a particular aspect of number meant as well as having a way of reaching their answer. Sometimes this approach seemed successful. For example, in the lesson on dividing by 3, most of the children were unable to do this until they were given a practical way of reaching the answer. At the end of the lesson and in subsequent lessons, many of the children were able to carry out simple divisions without use of objects. Like most strategies I saw, introducing ideas using practical activities did not work for everyone. The clearest example was Claire, who seemed to regard such activities as games rather than work. As will be seen in the next chapter, Claire actually performed better at standard written activities than she did on practical activities designed to precede them.

Individual preferences

For some children, practical equipment was useful not just when a new idea was introduced but for some time afterwards. An example is James. As explained in the last chapter, James preferred to use cubes for addition even when he was used to the idea and adults were encouraging him to move on to other methods. Although cubes seemed very useful to James, the same could not be said of money.

Money also presented difficulties for Julie, though these were less extreme. Sean, on the other hand, seemed very much at home dealing with money. Although practical work seemed to help most of the children, especially with new ideas, there was great variation both between individuals and according to the type of equipment.

Motivation

Another function of equipment is to provide motivation and interest, as suggested by the teachers interviewed by Moyer (2001). The teachers I worked with seemed to take a similar view and often the view seemed to be shared by the children. Some objects caused more interest than others, as can be seen from Sean's reaction to the pile of money. Very occasionally, the objects used were almost too interesting, as they provided a diversion, as in the case of toy cars. However, this was not true for the Smarties, which seemed to motivate the children without proving an impossible distraction. On the whole, everyday objects seemed to interest the children more than objects such as cubes, which were designed particularly for doing mathematics. It is also important to remember that other motivating factors were present in the practical lessons, as in other lessons. For example, it is possible that Matthew was motivated by the desire to make his measurements match his estimates and that Malcolm was motivated by a preference for working alone rather than with a girl.

Using and applying mathematics

The practical lessons I observed were less structured than many of the worksheet-based lessons which simply required the children to carry out a task over and over again. The practical lessons all offered more variety and tended to offer opportunities for decision-making and organisation of work, both considered by the English National Curriculum (DfEE and QCA 1999) to be aspects of using and applying mathematics. For example, the data-handling activity using dice required the children to organise a way of knowing when to stop. Many of them also devised a method of checking their results, which is also considered to be an aspect of using and applying mathematics. Problem-solving situations also arose, for example, in the incident where the floor was measured in nails or when Julie was trying to find a way of measuring her string. It is tempting to compare my observations with the views of some teachers who seemed to assume that by doing practical work they were automatically meeting the requirements of using and applying mathematics (SCAA 1993). Although I would argue that the connection was not automatic, nevertheless the detailed requirements of using and applying mathematics often did arise in practical sessions.

Number and other aspects of mathematics

Another important feature of practical lessons was that the vast majority of them covered important aspects of number even though they were often on other aspects of mathematics. For example, the issues of equivalence and conversion of units arose in discussion of centimetres and millimetres. Sometimes, as in the case of Lauren and the nails, children carried out harder calculations in practical lessons than they were working on in number lessons. Perhaps Lauren's correct answer could be seen as a maths fairy moment, as she performed at a higher level than usual. It is worth remembering, though, that I had no evidence that the children in this set could not double numbers like 63, but it was easy to assume that this would be the case from their difficulties with easier calculations.

Practical lessons also provided opportunities for children to practise basic numerical skills such as aspects of counting. This can be shown in Julie's attempts to count 2p, 5p and 10p coins. In Julie's case, these activities showed her difficulties with these aspects, which were less evident on written tasks. The data-handling activity using Smarties included opportunities for practice of counting objects and writing numbers. This was integrated in to the activity rather than being presented as revision of basic work.

The role of adults

Theoretical discussions on the place of practical work include disagreement about the role of instruction. For example, Wood (1988) points out that Piaget and Bruner have different views about the importance of instruction. I would like to widen this to the role of adults generally. In many of the incidents described, the mathematics did not automatically arise from the use of the equipment. The teachers had a crucial role in asking questions and in providing information. Sometimes activities were enhanced by the teacher not intervening too much, but allowing children to organise their own work or to select from the equipment provided.

Also crucial was the role of classroom assistants in observing the children's responses. Aplin (1998) points out that assistants can learn a lot about children from watching and listening to them. In adopting such a role with Julie, I was able to see how she went about counting money and thus understand her difficulties. Similarly, in many of the measuring activities, adult observation was crucial to see whether children were measuring accurately, as often answers were not known. My observations of measuring also raised the question about how useful estimation is. I discovered, like Ainley (1991) that some children simply put the final measurement down as an estimate. Perhaps more worrying was the case of Matthew, who actually measured incorrectly in order to reach an answer that matched his estimate.

Classroom suggestions

Observing and listening

My observations suggest that being near children when they are carrying out practical activities presents opportunities to see how they go about tasks and to observe their strengths and difficulties. Ask yourself:

- What strategies do children use when counting money? For example, can they count in twos, fives and tens? Can they count on from a starting point other than zero?
- Do children have strategies for measuring objects longer than the ruler?
- When children are measuring using non-standard units, do they use several objects or just one? If they use one, are they able to move it without gaps or overlaps?
- If children are asked to estimate before measuring, do they actually do this? If they have estimated, do they distort their measurements in order to reach an answer near the estimate?
- Do children use rulers correctly, starting at the right place and using the correct scale?

Planning and teaching

Here are some suggestions that teachers may consider when teaching and planning practical lessons:

- If some children do not respond to the practical introduction to a new aspect of work, it may be worth still presenting the work in another way rather than assuming they will not be able to do it.

- If estimation is used as part of your measuring, it is worth considering strategies for sharing and using estimates before the measuring is carried out.
- Exploit problem-solving situations which arise during practical activities.
- Offer opportunities to children to plan and organise their work.
- For shape activities, offer a wide variety of shapes.
- Exploit links between number and other topics, for example, measuring and data handling.

6   Written work

As the children came to the mat, the teacher remarked that they would be working in their books today. Claire said, 'I love sums, I love writing in my book.' The first task on the mat involved children being chosen to write on the board. After two children had been chosen, Claire said, 'I want a go.'

Introduction

This chapter concerns what I will loosely call written work, though 'recorded' might be more accurate, as writing of words was less common that recording numbers, symbols and calculations. Mostly this chapter is about children working from worksheets or in their maths books. The chapter will consider issues about recording mathematics including the writing of numbers and symbols and the use of written methods of calculation. My observations show that many children had difficulty with the reading and recording involved in written tasks and therefore performed poorly compared to their performance in similar tasks presented in an oral or mental way. For a small number of children, the opposite was the case and they actually did better on written tasks than on comparable practical or mental tasks. Standard written methods helped some children but appeared to confuse others. However, the same thing happened when a teacher introduced non-standard methods.

Background

Worksheets, schemes, textbooks in primary maths in England

In discussing changes in primary mathematics in England, Brown (1999) talks about commercial mathematics schemes. A key part of schemes were workbooks or textbooks for pupils to work through, and these were usually accompanied by guidance for teachers and supplementary materials. Such schemes were widely used in the 1970s and later and, as Brown says, many teachers stuck closely to the texts, often allowing pupils to work through them on their own. With the introduction of the National Curriculum in 1989 (DES 1989), teachers were less reliant on schemes to provide a framework for progression. This did encourage some variation in the way schemes were used (Millett and Johnson 1996). As Harries and Sutherland (1999) point out, schemes tend to be dismissed by experts, yet they are widely used.

Standard written methods

In discussing concerns about primary mathematics teaching in England raised in the early 1990s, Straker (1999) links the dominance of mathematics schemes with an over-emphasis on standard written methods. Research suggests that such methods can lead to particular problems for some children. For example, Yackel (2001) describes research in which American first- and second-grade pupils were asked to tackle the question $16 + 9$. First, the question was presented in a horizontal format where they were asked if they had a way to figure it out. The same question was then presented in vertical format in what looked like a page from a typical school workbook. Virtually all the children gave the correct answer of 25 to the question in the first format. Given the vertical format, a number of them attempted to remember procedures they had been taught. Although some children still obtained the correct answer of 25, others answered 15 or even 115.

Subtraction in vertical format using formal algorithms is also prone to problems. Hughes (1986) describes methods taught for column subtraction, saying that the method most popular in Britain at the time was the 'decomposition' method. He goes on to describe the problems some 8-year-old children had with this method. His main interest was in the difficulties children had in relating the method to the base ten blocks which were supposed to model it. Other difficulties he describes include problems with zero and smallest from largest. Ginsburg (1977) examines mistakes in school arithmetic. He says that these are often the result of faulty rules. He suggests that such rules have sensible origins and describes them as good rules badly applied or distorted to some degree. He also reports that some children seem to see arithmetic as an arbitrary game and are not concerned that different methods give different answers, failing to see one method as correct and the others as containing errors.

Written work in the National Numeracy Strategy

As discussed in earlier chapters, mental mathematics is considered central to the Numeracy Strategy. This means that written work assumes reduced importance, though it certainly does not disappear. The emphasis on whole-class teaching also means children are less likely to be working through books or schemes at 'their own pace' and therefore the amount of reading and recording they do is likely to be reduced.

The Strategy is accompanied by a booklet offering guidance on the teaching of written calculations (QCA 1999b), which lays out the expectations for children in each year group. Written methods have a low profile for the youngest children but the booklet states that the aim should be that by the end of Primary School children will have been taught and be secure with one standard method for each operation. *The National Numeracy Strategy: Framework for Teaching Mathematics* (DfEE 1999a) talks about jottings, informal written methods and standard written methods. Thompson (1999) considers these terms but offers a slightly different classification. The first type is 'informal non-standard written algorithms' which he describes as written expression of the children's thinking. He then distinguishes between 'formal standard' and 'formal non-standard' written algorithms. The term 'formal standard' is used for well-known methods such as 'decomposition', which he says are symbolic and contracted. In contrast, he claims 'formal non-standard' methods are more 'user-friendly' and based on ideas which underpin many of the informal mental strategies that children use. However, the methods are still classified as formal because they have a recognisable layout. Examples given include extended recording for addition and subtraction, where, for example, 358 is recorded as $300 + 50 + 8$ and the 'area' method for long multiplication which involves use of a diagram.

One concern about the current system is how children make the move from informal to formal written methods. For example, in a study of division methods, Anghileri *et al.* (2002) found that English pupils had difficulties that might stem from the fact that in England informal methods were simply replaced by formal methods.

Written work and individual needs

In discussing children's possible difficulties with mathematical tasks, Cockburn (1999) uses the phrase 'presentational complexity' to cover situations where tasks are presented in an inappropriate manner. She gives the example of worksheets covered in writing which could make it difficult for a child to know how to proceed. Advice about pupils with particular needs in the *Framework for Teaching Mathematics* (DfEE 1999a) acknowledges that reading difficulties or lack of familiarity with English can slow some children's progress with mathematics. It is therefore suggested that teachers should minimise any written instructions and explanations on worksheets and written exercises. It is acknowledged by Shuard and Rothery (1984) that at the time written communication was a major component of methods of teaching mathematics in most schools. They interpreted the word 'reading' in a wide sense as 'getting meaning from the page', a process which they say is influenced by style of writing, graphic images used and the presentation of the page.

In the classrooms

Many of the worksheets and exercises used had originally been designed as part of schemes, though the children were not expected to work through them independently. Instead, when written work was included, one particular sheet or set of calculations was given out, usually to all the pupils at the same time. The teacher explained most written work carefully before work started, with the teacher and other adults on hand to explain again in the case of difficulties. Occasionally, the teachers deliberately reduced the amount of instruction and help; usually this was when work was intended to perform an assessment function.

Both Year 5 sets made frequent use of worksheets. The children were occasionally asked to copy small amounts of writing or diagrams from the board. In the lower set, written work was carried out in almost every lesson in the form of either worksheets or calculations copied from the board. The children were also expected to be able to draw or copy charts and tables. Calculations were performed in a variety of ways and the children were allowed to carry out jottings on scrap paper. In the special needs set, the amount of recording children were expected to do on worksheets or in maths books was lower than in the other sets. In this set it was common for children to be allowed to record on the whiteboards.

Worksheets

The worksheets I saw fulfilled different purposes. Some were for completion at home, some were extra sheets for those who finished early and some were resource sheets, such as hundred squares. Most, however, were to be completed by all the children during the lesson. Some sheets were to be copied into maths books; some required the children to write answers on the sheets. The most common type of worksheets required children to carry out several calculations of the same type. Sometimes all the calculations followed exactly the same format. Sometimes the format varied slightly within the sheet. If this happened, the teachers usually explained carefully what was required in different parts of the sheet.

To a few children, the arrival of the sheet in front of them acted as a kind of starting gun in the race to completion. Sean, for example, invariably started the sheet as soon as he was given it, despite frequent instructions to the contrary. I once saw him try to write with the pencil almost horizontal in the hope that he wouldn't be noticed. On another occasion, he responded to the warning, '. . . no pencil in anyone's hand' by picking up a pen instead.

Despite Sean's enthusiasm for tackling sheets, he did not always complete them correctly. He had particular difficulty when he was required to copy the calculations from the sheet into his maths book. This was evident by observing his response to the introduction to work and comparing it to his written response. In the example below, I was sitting between Sean and Julie. First, the teacher introduced the idea of dividing by 2 and discussed some examples with the children. Later they carried out written work about dividing by 2:

> In the introductory part of the session, the teacher stressed the rationale for particular methods on the grounds that they would be needed when larger numbers were involved. To prove his point, the teacher said, 'What would you do if it was half of 286?' This was probably a rhetorical question, but Sean answered, 'Take away.' 'Take away what?' asked the teacher, to which Sean responded, 'One hundred . . . and . . . forty . . . three.' The teacher seemed surprised at Sean's ability to answer. The worksheet that followed involved dividing much smaller numbers by two. When it was distributed, Sean whispered, 'Oh no, not easy work again.' The teacher stipulated that the work be copied into books rather than completed on the sheet. He asked for children to copy two titles from the board and to write

each example in three ways, which he demonstrated on the board using the first example. Sean asked for my help in writing the titles and seemed to be slowed down more than the others by the requirements to record each calculation in three ways.

Although I helped Sean with the titles, Julie, who found the task really hard to begin with, then took most of my attention:

Julie did not seem to be able to make a start on the sheet. The teacher had made it clear that they could not use cubes or fingers and they could not use subtraction. Julie said she did not know any of her 2 times table, so I compromised by asking her if she could count in twos. She said she could and managed to count in twos to 12, using her fingers to keep track. I explained that this means that six twos make 12 and that six was the answer to the first division. Julie seemed happy with this method and decided to do the rest of the sheet in the same way. She found $24 \div 2$ harder because she had difficulty in counting in twos above 20. I helped her with this but Sean, who was on an earlier question, told her the correct answer.

My observations suggest that Sean had a good understanding of division by 2, even before the lesson started, while Julie found it very difficult. Looking at their finished work tells a different story. Julie was actually the first on our table and among the first in the room to have finished the sheet. She took it proudly to the teacher. At this point I looked at Sean's work. He was on question five while Julie had completed all twelve questions. Sean had incorrectly written $20 \div 2 = 9$. I said, 'Is that right?' and he said it was. I tried a different tack, saying, 'I bet you know in your head what half of 20 is.' He said, 'Oh yes,' grinned and changed it to 10.

The Year 5 teacher almost always explained worksheets step by step. Despite this, a frequent response to the arrival of the worksheets was some anxiety about what was expected. Comments such as, 'Tell me what to do', or 'I don't know what to do', were frequent. Towards the end of the year, when I was becoming familiar with the reactions of various children to worksheets, they were given a sheet that produced a quite different response. The sheet in question, which I will call the 'chicken and egg sheet', was actually given to the children face down so they could use the back for scrap paper when working out calculations. The sheets had come from a pile of imperfect copies of French worksheets, designed for older children, abandoned by the photocopier. The pictures were of chickens and eggs, but the instructions were in French. The children's response to the sheet is described here:

> The instruction not to turn the sheet over was too much for many to resist and it soon became known that there was an interesting picture on the back. Towards the end of the lesson the teacher relented and said they could turn the sheet over, but most had done so before then. On our table, a discussion soon started on what the sheet was about and what you had to do. Each part of the picture was numbered and the top of the sheet carried what looked like a key. Many of the words were not familiar, but 'bleu' and 'brun' confirmed the suspicion that they might be colours. The children were now fairly confident that the sheet had to be coloured using the numbers and the key to tell you which section was which colour. With blue and brown identified, it remained to work out the others. 'Rouge', it was felt, probably meant red, but the others were not recognisable. Then someone had the idea of working backwards from the picture. Find the number on the grass and that would be green; similarly the chicken was bound to be yellow. Soon the key was cracked and those who wanted to could take the sheet home to colour it in.

Talking to the other adults afterwards confirmed that the children on the other tables had reacted in a similar way. This was in marked contrast to the way they usually responded to maths sheets, with a desire to have everything explained and checked and a reluctance to work things out for themselves.

Working from Boards

In all the classrooms, there was at least one whiteboard or blackboard at the front of the room. These were used frequently by the teacher for explaining and demonstrating. Other uses varied between the classes. These included copying from the board and copying examples from the board to complete in maths books. Children were also sometimes asked to write on the boards themselves. Of all the activities using boards, copying from the board was probably the least popular with the children:

> When the test was over, the teacher moved on to talking about place value, which it appeared they had started work on the day

before. The initial task was to make numbers, using the digits 1, 2 and 6. After this, maths books were given out and the children were asked to copy some writing from the blackboard. The heading was 'Place Value'. Underneath was written, 'Each number is made from digits. There are ten digits, 0, 1, 2, 3, 4, 5, 6, 7, 8 and 9. The position of a digit gives its value.' Copying from the blackboard seemed to present some difficulty to all the boys I was sitting with. I helped them by writing the title on my pad so they could copy from there rather from the board. With help, they did manage the task, but it took some time. Adrian was particularly reluctant to do the task, saying that it was stupid.

Although many children were reluctant to copy from the board, this was not always the case. In one lesson Damian copied some diagrams from the board onto a notepad, although he hadn't been asked to. The lesson was about multiplying two-digit numbers by single-digit numbers using what the teacher called the grid method:

The teacher drew a grid on the board for the calculation 15×7. Damian, who was sitting next to me, copied this grid onto a sheet of my notepad. I was surprised to see how different his grid was from the one he was copying. The teacher filled in the answer to the calculation and Damian copied this also. For the next calculation, Damian again drew a grid much bigger than was needed. When he tried to copy the grid for the next calculation, which was 22×14, I tried to encourage him to draw it with the same number of boxes as the teacher. This time he was closer, but he drew a 2 by 4 grid instead of a 3 by 3. I pointed out that one of the numbers was in the wrong place, but Damian didn't seem to think that mattered.

All of Damian's diagrams were different to those he was apparently copying. This can be seen by looking at Figure 6.1 which shows the three diagrams the teacher drew on the board with Damian's copies alongside them.

I didn't know why Damian's first diagrams were so different from the ones he was supposed to be copying. Perhaps he had simply drawn the grids without paying attention to the number of rows and columns. Certainly, when I prompted him to think about the size, he drew something nearer to that drawn by the teacher, but even this diagram contained a crucial mistake. Damian was not using the sides

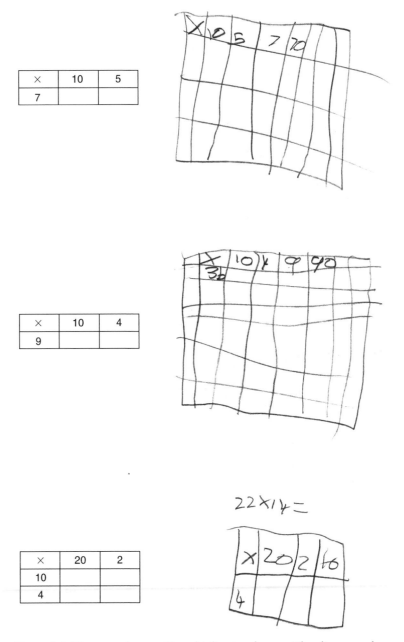

×	10	5
7		

×	10	4
9		

×	20	2
10		
4		

Figure 6.1 Diagrams from grid multiplication lesson. The diagrams drawn on the board by the teacher are shown on the left, Damian's 'copies' are shown on the right

of the grid to show the two numbers he was multiplying split into parts. His diagrams did not show a physical representation of the multiplication in the way that had been intended.

Writing on boards

Writing on boards was a particularly frequent activity in the special needs set. There were two whiteboards in the classroom, which were often used for optional activities at the start of the lesson. These sometimes took the form of completing or writing number patterns or sequences. Some children seemed particularly keen on this activity. For example, Ben often chose work on the whiteboards:

> Ben was writing sequences of numbers on the board. He started at 10 and increased in tens to 190. All the numbers were written correctly and he could read them out. Then he started writing large numbers, including 1000, and correctly read them to the teacher. Next, he started a new sequence going up in fives. The sequence started 5, 10, 51. When asked to read the numbers, Ben said, 'Five, ten, fifteen.'

Other children in the class also made occasional mistakes in writing numbers. Douglas and Neil both sometimes confused the order of digits in teens numbers in the same way as Ben did. Children also sometimes had problems with writing larger numbers.

Working in maths books

In all the sets, children sometimes completed work in their mathematics books. This was often copied either from sheets, workbooks or the blackboard. Claire was a particularly enthusiastic user of books, as can be seen from her comment at the start of the chapter, which was made fairly late in the year. The incident below took place two weeks after the lesson reported in the last chapter where Claire had apparent difficulty adding the spots on dominoes:

> The children were asked to write the date and the title, 'Make Ten', in their maths books. Claire was one of several children who had a problem at this point. She was worried about putting dots in the date. I moved to help Michael, who had not written anything at all. He asked me to write the title for him. The task was to write number sentences starting from $10 + 0 = 10$ fol-

lowed by $9 + 1 = 10$ and continuing to $0 + 10 = 10$. I worked with Michael and we used a tower of cubes, moving one over each time. Mostly, Michael counted the cubes but when we got to $1 +$, I noticed he knew the next number was 9 without counting. Claire, meanwhile, carried out the activity without adult help. At the end, the children took their books to the mat. An error was spotted in Claire's work and she went back to the table to correct it. She had mistakenly written a 9 in the column of tens. She re-wrote the answer, putting the 10 in one square. She then rubbed it out, putting the one and zero in separate squares, as she had with the other tens. Then, she started to rewrite every calculation next to the first one so each line of her book contained the same calculation written twice. I tried to persuade her to stop this without success. She finished and went to show her book to the teacher. She was very proud of it.

This incident can be seen in a positive light as it showed that Claire was quite capable of carrying out the additions that she had not done practically two weeks before. The fact that she had reached 9 for one of the totals is puzzling. I was not with Claire when she reached the answers, but it is possible that she found the total each time by counting both sets of cubes, not realising that it would always be ten. Although Claire was keen on work of this type, it did not seem to be the mathematical ideas which received her attention. Instead, she focused on details like the date, rubbing out carefully, writing neatly and putting digits in separate squares.

Standard written methods

Standard written methods were used most in the Year 5 sets. The Year 5 teacher seemed to have a preference for standard written methods and in particular he preferred to write calculations in vertical rather than horizontal format. Some examples of this have been given in earlier chapters, including Penny's response described in Chapter 1. Although calculations were usually presented in a written format and out of context, they did occasionally arise from contexts or problems. One such problem was about sports shirts:

The teacher established that they needed to add 22 and 59 to solve the problem and a volunteer was sought to do this. Lawrence came to the board to explain how to do it. He started by saying, 'You get the fifties and you get the twenties.' The teacher suggested writing the calculation down as a standard addition. Later, the children were looking at numbers of cotton shirts and comparing the number of white shirts and blue shirts. The teacher asked how many more. Bryn answered 5 and the teacher asked how he did it. Bryn said, 'I just counted on from 17 to 22,' then Bob said, 'I just knew it.' Later, someone else suggested '. . . or you could take away'. The next example involved comparing 59 with 84. I encouraged Bryn to try this question but he said he '. . . can't be bothered'. The teacher showed the children how to do the calculation on the board using subtraction in vertical format.

In this incident, the teacher asked the children what methods they used, but when it came to explaining a harder example, he used the vertical method. This meant that children such as Bryn, using other methods, either had to work out for themselves how to extend the method to harder numbers or had to abandon their method.

Formal non-standard methods

In the lower set, the teacher often demonstrated formal non-standard methods of calculation. The first lesson I saw like this was about addition of two-digit numbers. The children had been introduced to this method the day before but the teacher reminded them of it before giving them some more examples to do:

The example on the blackboard was written in horizontal format. It was:

$$33 + 14 + 17 + 26$$

The children talked through the method they had used the previous day. This involved finding pairs of units to total 10. The 3 was linked with 7 and the 4 was linked with 6. It was then simply a case of adding multiples of 10. We went back to our places to do the examples from the board. All the children I was working with had some difficulty in seeing and copying from the board. The next problem was that the children did not seem to know by heart pairs of numbers to total 10. We worked some of these out together and wrote them on a pad as a reminder. Even given this help, the children still had difficulties. Sarah told me she had the answer 20 for the first calculation, which was:

$11 + 23 + 19 + 17$

Sarah did not seem worried that this answer was smaller than one of the numbers she had started with. When she started to explain her method, it became clear that she was mentally adding tens, and then later treating them as units. Next, I helped Damian. We used a jotting pad to do the first calculation. We joined pairs of units to total 10, then worked out the total numbers of tens using tally marks. We arrived at the correct answer of 70. I then left Damian to do the next example on the pad. His jottings, shown in Figure 6.2, indicate that he had difficulty with this. The calculation was:

$42 + 11 + 18 + 9$

Damian arrived at the answer 20, though it was hard to see how from his jottings. His jottings also indicated that he did not realise you could not add tens to units in this way. Another

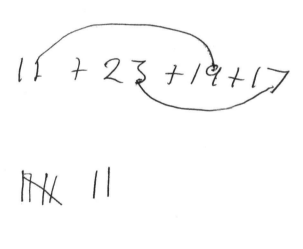

Figure 6.2 Damian's jottings from addition lesson

difficulty the children had was that they could not mentally add multiples of 10. This can be seen in the unnamed jottings shown in Figure 6.3. In the example shown, the child had to write 70, 10 and 10 underneath each other in order to add them. The final jottings on this sheet are not easy to explain.

By the end of the lesson, some of the children in our group had made some progress. Tony and Damian both managed to do the first five with some help. Miriam, in contrast, did three examples, getting only one right. She told me the teacher had done this for her. She got 79 instead of 80 for one question.

Discussion

Task preferences

For many of the children I worked with, the way a task was presented, for example practical, oral or written, made a difference to their response. For some children, this difference was great. Some children had difficulty in copying titles from the board and in setting

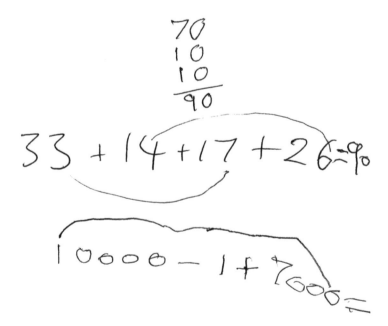

Figure 6.3 Un-named jottings from an addition lesson

out calculations on paper and some were also hampered by difficulties in reading written instructions or questions, or in drawing charts and tables. A few still had occasional problems in writing numbers correctly, though this tended to be an intermittent rather than consistent problem. As the case of Ben illustrates, lack of consistency in writing low numbers did not necessarily mean children were unable to progress to reading and writing higher numbers.

Sometimes children made whispered comments about their difficulty with tasks or how they felt about them. Some were open about their difficulties, some, like Adrian, talked instead about tasks being stupid. As I got to know Adrian, I realised that he found copying from the board very difficult. He did complete the task, albeit reluctantly. There were other occasions when children apparently refused to do such tasks. Sometimes, I discovered that children apparently declining to do work would slowly cooperate when offered help with the reading or recording. Thus they appeared to be opting out of the task deliberately, but their refusal often masked genuine difficulties. I call this 'tactical opting out', which is described in more detail elsewhere (Houssart 2002a).

Although many children had difficulties with written tasks, it is important to remember that some children were better at them than at oral or practical tasks. A clear example of this is Julie. In part, this can be explained by the fact that she did not experience difficulties with reading, writing or drawing charts in the way that many of the children did. It also seems that the format of the worksheets assisted her. She showed a preference for a procedural way of working that involved knowing how to do the first question, then doing all the others in exactly the same way. Usually, her knowledge about the first question came directly from an adult. In this way, Julie seemed able to overcome some of her difficulties in working with number and often completed worksheets ahead of others in the class who showed a deeper understanding.

Although children who had difficulty with writing and drawing tended to avoid such tasks, there were exceptions. An example of this can be seen in Damian's difficulty with copying grids from the board. He often drew or copied charts or diagrams when he had not been asked to, as was the case in this lesson. In this case, the difficulty seemed to be perceptual rather than physical. Damian's difficulty seemed to be in reproducing the grids in the way the teacher had drawn them. His diagrams suggest that this method of multiplication was unlikely to make sense to him. The method is based on the idea that a physical model will show children how the numbers are broken down. Although this sort of diagram may make the situation clear to many children, this did not seem to be the case for Damian.

A slightly different example is Claire. She did not necessarily answer incorrectly when given practical or oral tasks, but she did sometimes fail to engage with such tasks. Claire had a history of challenging behaviour. She had some bad days when she came to the room apparently unwilling to co-operate. However, even on bad days, close observation suggests that she was more willing to co-operate when written work was involved.

Methods of calculation

Children sometimes had preferences for certain methods of calculation. Sean and Lawrence, for example, avoided standard methods. Often, it seemed to be the case that those who willingly used standard methods were those like Julie, with a preference for written work. Those who preferred less standard methods were often those who showed a preference for working orally.

Julie and Sean's teacher had a preference for standard written methods. It is possible that a different approach based on a development of mental methods might have been easier for Sean. Some of the other teachers had a different approach to calculations, which was more in line with the numeracy project and with what Thompson (1999) calls 'formal non-standard methods'. Sarah and Damian's teacher often used this approach. As with the more formal approach, it seemed that some children were helped by it but others had difficulties.

The method of adding two-digit numbers using pairs to 10 is an example. This method seems to have been of limited use to the group of children I was with. Although it was designed to reflect a mental method, it seems unlikely that any of these children used such a method. It was built on the assumption that it was relatively easy to recall pairs of numbers which total 10 and to add multiples of 10. Neither of these things were the case for this group of children. In addition, the method led to some of the errors associated with formal methods such as confusing tens with units and not reflecting on whether the answer made sense.

My observations of children using standard methods are in line with those of others (Ginsburg 1977; Hughes 1986; Yackel 2001) who suggest that they often apply rules in a faulty way and do not particularly expect methods to make sense. However, I found that for some children, very similar things happened when formal non-standard methods were used. These methods may be beneficial when they are an extension of the child's own preferred mental methods. However, when they were taught to the whole class, they seemed to become just another standard method with all the associated pitfalls.

Written instructions

My observations suggest that many children had some difficulty in reading and interpreting written instructions, something the teachers were certainly aware of. A common response to reading and related difficulties was to reduce written instructions as much as possible, to make sure everything was explained by adults and to present work in which the same idea was repeated several times. The chicken and egg sheet was an exception to this. In this case, children showed tenacity in working out what to do and in trying out ideas in marked contrast to their usual expectation that everything would be explained. This was one of the maths fairy moments when I felt there were several possible explanations for the children's success.

One possible explanation is that the children felt no pressure to produce a correct solution to the chicken and egg sheet. Maths sheets, in contrast, were always going to be marked and commented on which might have made children less willing to take a risk with them. Perhaps the chicken and egg sheet proved particularly motivating. This could have been because of the attractive picture, but it may have been because it contained a challenging task designed for older children or even because it was 'forbidden'. Another possibility is that the routines established in the classroom to support the children had unwittingly added to their dependency. There was an expectation that everything would be explained step by step by the teacher and that additional help would be provided on request by the other adults in the room.

The chicken and egg sheet suggests that there may be dangers in always ensuring that instructions on worksheets are very simple and clearly explained. One unintended consequence of this may have been the unwillingness of some children to try to work things out for themselves. Another consequence was the tendency for tasks to be very straightforward and sometimes repetitive. The consequences of this are discussed in a later chapter.

Classroom suggestions

Observing and listening

My observations suggest that individual children often have particular difficulties with aspects of written work as well as having preferences for or against particular methods or recording in general. Those working in classrooms may want to look for the following:

- Children with difficulties in writing or copying from the board.
- Children who copy charts and tables incorrectly.
- Children who need help in reading instructions.
- Children showing a strong preference for or against written work.
- Children with particular enthusiasm for certain taught methods.
- Children using alternative methods of calculation to those taught.

Planning and teaching

Whatever the approach and preference of the teacher, there are some children who are likely to be disadvantaged. Although there is no simple solution, offering more variety and flexibility may go some way towards assisting the children. Some suggestions follow:

- Vary the way work is presented so that children work on the same idea mentally, practically and in written form. This will also allow comparison of how children approach the same work presented in different ways.
- Be aware of differences in preferred methods of calculation. Encourage children to share their methods and allow them to complete written work using a method that suits them.
- When methods are being extended, for example to cater for larger numbers, bear in mind that those using alternative methods may need help in extending their own methods.
- When worksheets or other instructions are given out, encourage children to work alone or together to try to decide what is required.
- For some children, explicit discussion of charts and tables might help, including a consideration of how many rows or columns there are and why.

7 Calculators and computers

Year 5 children were working on a calculator investigation which involved dividing multiples of 3 by 3. Some children also carried out calculations not suggested by the teacher and there was some unofficial swapping of decimal answers. Adrian did 100 divided by 3 on his calculator and proudly showed it to me, saying, 'Got another one.'

Introduction

This chapter deals with tasks for which the children used calculators or, in a few cases, computers. The background reading section suggests that at the time of the study, use of calculators and computers was low in many English primary schools. My observations confirm that this was the case in the schools I worked in. Despite this, some conclusions about calculator use are possible. The first is that many children had difficulty carrying out apparently simple tasks with a calculator. The second is that calculator use sometimes led children to investigate apparently complex aspects of mathematics and to make discoveries. Calculators particularly suited some children and my limited observations suggest that this was also true of computers.

Background

History of calculator use

Calculators have had a chequered history in English primary schools, resulting in a fairly low level of use at the time of this study. The Cockcroft Report, published in 1982, drew attention to the impact that the availability of calculators might have on the mathematics curriculum, suggesting the possibility of a 'calculator aware curriculum' (Cockroft 1982). This was followed by materials suggesting ways calculators might be used (e.g. Mathematical Association 1987; Open University 1982) and a large curriculum development project, carried out with 6–9-year-olds, known as the calculator aware number project or CAN (Shuard *et al.* 1991).

The CAN project ended as the National Curriculum was introduced (DES 1989). Although this included some provision for calculator use, especially in the non-statutory guidance, this fell far short of the work carried out in the CAN project. In tracing the development of calculator use following CAN, Ruthven (2001) suggests that calculator use in English primary schools, following the introduction of the National Curriculum, was low. This view was supported by inspection evidence, which suggested limited calculator use (SCAA 1997). Ruthven (1999) also suggests that the use of calculators in primary schools became increasingly contentious and the phrase 'calculator beware' was a better description of the approach to calculators in many schools than the 'calculator aware' once intended.

Recent developments

The introduction of the National Numeracy Strategy has done little to change this. Although the *Framework for Teaching Mathematics* (DfEE 1999a) describes the calculator as a 'powerful and efficient tool', its use is only openly advocated for 9–11-year-olds. However, it concedes that calculators offer a unique way of learning about numbers and the number system and it also suggests that children need to be taught the technical skills of calculator use. A mixed picture of calculator use is confirmed by early evaluation of the National Numeracy Strategy (OFSTED 2000). This suggests that many teachers lacked confidence in using calculators as a teaching aid and teaching pupils how to make the best use of them. However, the report indicates a relatively high level of calculator use in Years 5 and 6 with about one-quarter of the lessons observed with these year groups including some use of calculators. One possible factor in maintaining the use of calculators towards the end of primary schools is national testing. National Curriculum Tests require children to use calculators in one of the written papers, and feedback from the tests (QCA 2000) recommends that children be encouraged to use calculators in appropriate situations.

Ways of using calculators

The National Numeracy Strategy: Framework for Teaching Mathematics (DfEE 1999a) gives examples of how 9–11-year-olds might use calculators. About half of the activities are concerned with developing the skills of calculator use. The majority of the others concern calculating with realistic data in problem-solving situations. Other sources contain more detail about using calculators to enhance children's understanding of number. For example, Rousham and Rowland (1996) suggest that the calculator can act as a 'cognitive reorganiser', allowing the user to conceptualise number in a different way. In a recent book entitled *Teaching Number Sense*, Anghileri (2000) makes frequent mention of calculators, including a section about using calculators to motivate and empower children. One area of mathematics in which calculator activities are advocated is the understanding of multiplication and division (BECTa 2001). They also have potential in assisting children's understanding of place value, large numbers, negative numbers and decimals (Shuard *et al.* 1991). In addition, they are useful for generating sequences of numbers using what is known as the constant function. This is described by the Open University (1982) as an extremely powerful teaching tool.

Low attainers and calculators

A study carried out in one local education authority involved in the CAN project (Rowland 1994) questioned whether the lowest-attaining children benefited from calculator access. However, some CAN teachers pointed out that they had noticed an improved attitude to mathematics in these children (Rousham and Rowland 1996). The book based on the CAN project (Shuard *et al.* 1991) contains some examples of incidents where children considered to be low attainers surprised their teachers. Possible difficulties in using calculators are also evident. For example, they quote from a low-attaining 8-year-old who did $16 \div 3$ on a calculator correctly, but thought the answer was wrong. In a more recent study of 10- and 11-year-olds, Ruthven and Chaplin (1997) noted a tendency for low attainers to misformulate divisions on a calculator by reversing the order of numbers, or to misinterpret the decimal answers.

Computers

The history of computer use in primary mathematics is outlined by Fox *et al.* (2000) who point to wide differences in use between and even within schools. They also suggest five categories of mathematics software: drill and practice, integrated learning systems, maths adventure and problem-solving, Logo and data handling. Over the years there have been enthusiastic advocates of software such as Logo, databases and spreadsheets and advice and suggestions for teachers have been available (e.g. Ainley 1996; NCET 1997). Despite this, recent reports suggest a low level of computer use in primary mathematics lessons. OFSTED (2001) report low computer use in the daily mathematics lesson, with the most common use being as a stand-alone activity enabling pupils to practise number bonds or other skills. The Numeracy Strategy only advocates this type of use if the computer activity is consistent with the lesson objectives (DfEE 1999a).

In the classrooms

During my three years of classroom observation I saw calculators used in six lessons. In half of these lessons, the main role of the calculator was for checking. I also saw them used for dealing with 'real data', for investigating the relationship between multiplication and division and to generate sequences of numbers. Fortunately, although use was limited, when it did occur, it was usually for the whole lesson and I was usually well placed to observe and listen to the children. For this reason, the rest of this chapter deals mainly with incidents of calculator use.

Computer use was also low and was observed in only two of the sets. The special needs set spent two lessons in the computer room and in addition to this, computers were used in the classroom during five lessons. In the lower set, the computers were almost always available to children for use before school. They were also available for those who completed their work early and the teacher often chose a programme related to their work for this purpose. On a few occasions, children used computers during the main part of the lesson. I was not always in a position to observe children as they used the computers usually because I was working with those engaged in other tasks. The incidents used in this chapter are drawn from the few occasions when I was able to observe computer use.

Using calculators

The first calculator lesson I saw was with a Year 5 set. The initial focus of the activity was to perform straightforward calculations with a calculator. The teacher then moved to using larger numbers in a context:

> The teacher asked the children to do 57 – 14 using the calculators. On the table where I was working, only Rashina managed to do this and there seemed to be a similar picture across the room. The next problem was to find the difference between 196 and 72. After that, problems were presented in context. To the amusement of some of the class, the teacher announced that Mrs Wilson, one of the classroom assistants, wanted to buy a new car, a Ford Fiesta costing £8,294. Her husband was going to give her some money to do this. She already had £5,684; the problem was to work out how much more she needed. Even before the teacher articulated the problem, I heard Darren say in a whisper, 'She's three thousand short.' Working this out with the calculator proved very difficult and the children seemed to need help in knowing which keys to press. I helped Linda and together we got the correct answer, as did Rashina. The teacher gave the correct answer and asked how many had got it right. Six children in the room claimed to have done this, including the two sitting with me. The next problem was a similar one, and for the first time Erica sought my help, pointing to the keys of the calculator and asking, 'Which is take-away?'

I was surprised at how many incorrect answers were obtained using calculators. I was also interested in the performance of individuals. Rashina, for example, had been one of a small number of children to get the right answer, which was unusual for her. I wondered whether this success would be sustained in other calculator lessons. There were other positive aspects of the lesson. Darren's comment, 'She's three thousand short', suggested that he had rounded the numbers and performed a mental calculation to give an approximate answer.

Checking with calculators

Soon after the lesson described above, the same children used calculators for another subtraction task. The task started with a reminder of how to use calculators for subtraction and then most of the lesson was spent using calculators to check subtractions done using written methods. For most children, this meant writing the subtractions in columns and using decomposition. The following incidents are drawn from this lesson:

> Linda had written a column subtraction in her maths book. It was $1,999 - 1,000$. She carried this out digit-by-digit, starting with the units, and arrived at the answer 999. She said to me, 'I don't think that's right,' but added, 'Don't tell me.' She checked with the calculator and was surprised to find that she was right.

> Wesley was working at the other side of the table. He was reminded of the task by the teacher and at one point asked to start again. I was fairly certain that he was not carrying out the calculations using a standard written method but instead was using the calculator under the table.

The children in the special needs set also used the calculator as a check. Sometimes this was a check to calculations done mentally, sometimes they were asked to check written calculations using a calculator. One such task involved the addition of three numbers. The numbers involved were relatively small. For example, the first calculation required the children to add 8, 2 and 3:

> I was sitting with four children, Kate, Neil, Seth and Adam. Kate followed the instructions exactly, doing each calculation without the calculator and writing the answer before checking with the calculator. The three boys were more inclined to start by using the calculator, though eventually Seth realised that he could do some of the calculations faster without.

Investigating multiplication and division

Calculators were also used to support other work, such as understanding the relationship between multiplication and division. One of the Year 5 sets spent most of a lesson using calculators to investigate multiplication and division by 3:

> The lesson started with a discussion of the 3 times table. The teacher demonstrated that multiples of 3 could be identified by adding the digits. Soon after this, calculators were given out and switched on. Nadeem, who was sitting next to me, showed me

the M in the display and asked me how to get rid of it. I showed him how to do this and was soon doing the same for others on the table. At the same time I noticed that Adrian had discovered that repeatedly pressing equals after a calculation changed the answer. The teacher asked us to test some numbers to see if they were multiples of 3. I worked with Matthew and Nadeem on this and they soon seemed to manage the activity.

The teacher then changed the activity to division and started by asking, 'How many groups of 3 are in 3?' Next they were asked to do 6 ÷ 6 on the calculator. Bryn got very excited about getting the answer 1, though he had difficulty in explaining what he had noticed. He then did the next calculation directed by the teacher, 9 ÷ 9 and announced his discovery, 'Everything related to the 3 or the 6, the answer is 1.' One of the girls at the back of the room seemed to be muttering an alternative discovery but unfortunately I could not hear the details and the teacher did not pick it up. Meanwhile, Matthew used his calculator to do 5 ÷ 5, a calculation not suggested by the teacher. He got the answer 1 but didn't tell anyone.

At this point, quite a lot of pressing had been going on other than that directed by the teacher. Early in the activity, Lawrence shouted out that he'd got 'minus 00979'. A bit later, Matthew claimed to have done 9 divided by 6 on the calculator and got the answer 15. He then did 5 ÷ 3 correctly but thought the answer must be wrong. The teacher continued to highlight the connection between multiplication and division, writing 9 × 3 = 27 on the board and asking the children to do 27 ÷ 3 on their calculators. Matthew said, 'I want to do it a different way' and did 3 ÷ 27 instead. The lesson continued in this way with a mixture of official and unofficial calculations and a mixture of correct and incorrect answers. At one point Matthew showed me the result of dividing 3 by 9 on the calculator. He tried to read the answer out, and said, 'It's weird.' A little later, probably after further experimentation, Matthew showed me that his calculator had an E in the display and he asked me to get rid of it.

Decimals, particularly recurring decimals, frequently arose in this lesson. This was not part of the teacher-intended activity, but became a focus for many children. Although confused by the decimals, they were also intrigued. As the story at the beginning of the chapter illustrates, they seemed to recognise these numbers as a category and started to predict which calculations might give such answers.

Generating sequences

The children in the special needs set used calculators to generate number sequences. On the basic calculators that they used, this was relatively easy to do either by pressing the add key twice or by repeatedly pressing the equals key. I was not present when the teacher first showed the children how to do this, but I was there the following day. The three incidents that follow all occurred on that day:

> As soon as the children came into the classroom, they were given a sheet about numbers missing from sequences. The first sequence was 5, 10, __, 20. The children were also given calculators. Douglas immediately used the constant function for the first sequence. He pressed $5 + + =$ to generate multiples of 5, then correctly filled in the missing number, 15.

> A bit later, I moved to sit near Claire, who was working on the same sheet. She made some use of the calculator but made mistakes in doing this. She kept turning round and writing on the whiteboard behind her. When she got to the harder examples, such as 16, 14, __, 10, she tried to use the constant function on the calculator to help her. This proved quite difficult and I started to show her how to do it. She cleared what I had done on the calculator and restarted (incorrectly) herself. Because the sequences she was working on were decreasing rather than increasing and because of the different starting points, the strategy used for simple sequences would not work here. Claire was undeterred. She was faced with the sequence 15, 12, __, 6. She used her calculator to enter $15 + 12 =$. She got the answer 27 and put this in the space. She seemed happy with the resulting sequence 15, 12, 27, 6.

> After some short counting activities the teacher asked the children about the word 'multiple' and about the work they had done the day before with the calculator. Douglas put his hand up and said, 'You put the 2 in and you press add two times and you press equals.' He was congratulated on this answer and told he would get a star.

These incidents suggest that for Douglas at least, using the calculator was a very positive experience. This was not true for Claire, who has been shown in previous chapters to have a strong preference for written work. Some children also seemed to have preferences for and against computer use, which is dealt with below.

Using computers

Sometimes children worked at the computers with their teacher while I was working with other children on a different task assigned by the teacher. At the end of one such lesson, Douglas, who had been working on the computers, came to talk to me. I asked him about the computer and the teacher suggested that he could show me during playtime. Douglas agreed and we actually spent the whole of playtime at the computer:

> Douglas showed me the program he had been working on. He explained clearly what you have to do to start with and as we progressed he added further explanations about the aim of the game. The program involved giving answers to sums such as $5 + 3$, $4 + 2$. Douglas got them all right, mostly using a number line. Then he decided to try a higher level. He had been on Level 1 but now went to Level 15. The first calculation was 11×12. He exited from this and tried to find another program, but most of them wouldn't start.

This was typical of the activities set up for children to use on the classroom computers. A drill and practice program was provided, designed to fit closely with the work the children were doing. The teacher selected the program and in this case the level. When the children worked in the computer room, the computers were used in a slightly different way. On the first occasion, they were used for data-handling purposes, on the second occasion they were used to access the Internet. The second occasion involved children being instructed to visit a particular site where drill and practice programs were provided. Parts of the data-handling lesson are described below:

> Before the lesson, the computers in the computer room were set up with the program the children were going to use. This was a program called *Starting Graph*, which presented numerical data in various graphical forms including pictograms. In a previous lesson, the children had done a survey of party food and they

brought with them lists of numbers ready to put in the computer to draw graphs. Some children completed this task very easily. Quam Nam found the work particularly easy and though I talked him through all the extensions I could think of, it seemed difficult to produce work that would stretch him using this program. Kate and James also completed the task well. Other children were harder to keep on task, for example Claire. Seth seemed to have a bad day, on several occasions he did not do as he was asked and pressed incorrect keys. He was assisted by myself and other adults but when left without an adult tended to exit from the work he had been started on.

The computer lessons, like calculator lessons, raised difficulties and minor distractions for some children. These are described in more detail in the following section.

Difficulties

A small but frequent distraction in calculator lessons was the appearance of M or E in the display. Children sometimes asked me to get rid of these letters, though they did not seem to distinguish between them or to realise that the E invalidated the answer in the display while the M didn't.

Some of the children seemed to have other difficulties with calculator use. These fell broadly into three areas. The first was difficulty with the operation keys containing the symbols for add, subtract, multiply and divide. The second difficulty was in reading numbers from the display, and the third was in double or incorrect pressing of keys. Some of the incidents described already suggest problems with operation keys. Erica asked me to identify the 'take away' key fairly late on during that activity, though this could partially be explained by her difficulties with spoken English. It is likely that Matthew also pressed the wrong operation key when claiming to do 9 divided by 6 and get the answer 15. Another area that presented difficulties for some children was reading the answer from the calculator display:

> The children were supposed to be doing additions then checking with the calculator. I suspected that Neil was using the calculator first. I asked him about the calculation he was on and he said that the answer was 20. He did not seem to believe me when I said that the answer was too high. I asked him to redo the calculation and he did so reluctantly. When he showed me the answer

on his calculator, I realised that he had got the correct answer 12 but was reading it as 20.

The final area of difficulty was in mispressing or double-pressing keys. Sometimes children pressed a key twice, resulting either in the wrong number, for example, 33 instead of 3, or in the calculator carrying out a calculation twice, for example, when they pressed the equals key twice. On other occasions children simply pressed the wrong key:

Jed was having problems subtracting 79 from 101. When the teacher asked if anyone had another answer besides 22, Jed replied that he did. Jed had co-ordination problems and it seems likely that he had accidentally pressed the equals key twice, meaning that the calculator had subtracted twice, leaving him with a negative answer. This may well have been accidental, but I noticed that as the lesson continued Jed continued to keep pressing the equals key and seemed quite interested in the answers.

Difficulties also arose when children were using computers. Many children seemed to have difficulty typing in web addresses when they were using the Internet. Part of this lesson is described here:

At the beginning of the session, one of the classroom assistants demonstrated what the children had to do using a computer connected to a large screen. This included typing in a password, double-clicking on *Internet Explorer* and typing in the web address given. I sat between Seth and Claire. Both needed a lot of help with the address, especially finding the letter keys. There was confusion between the names of letters and their sounds. Seth seemed to find this particularly hard. He had problems distinguishing between G and J and between E and I. He also made quite a few mistakes. Claire got onto the site first. Seth's computer did not seem to work so he moved to another computer and got on eventually. Meanwhile, Claire clicked on the wrong thing and exited from the site. I helped her get back in.

Talking to the other adults afterwards confirmed that many of the other children had similar difficulties. I was particularly interested in Seth's difficulty, which may have been related to the fact that English was not his first language. His difficulty in this lesson made me rethink his behaviour the previous week in the data-handling lesson. There had been an assumption among the adults that Seth was not co-operating in this lesson, but it is possible that he had genuine difficulty with the computer keys. It is also possible that he was reacting in a similar way to children who had difficulty in copying from the board. In other words, he preferred to be seen as refusing to do the task rather than as unable to do it and in need of help.

Discoveries

In the incident described earlier when Jed was using the calculator, his difficulty turned into a discovery as he realised that interesting things happened if you kept pressing the equals key. As the lesson continued, Wesley, sitting nearby, became interested in what Jed was doing and started to do something similar himself:

> As the teacher moved on to the next task, Wesley continued to press keys on his calculator. At one point, he appeared to copy down a number from the calculator on the back of a digit card. The teacher started to introduce the written task, which was to do a page of subtractions using a standard written method then check the results using a calculator. The teacher admonished Wesley for turning round and whispering to the boy behind him. Wesley said, 'I was telling him something about maths,' but the teacher did not reply. As the books were given out later, Wesley told me what he had been whispering about. He showed me that repeatedly pressing the equals key changes the answer. I asked what was happening and he explained by clearing the calculator, entering the number 3 and repeatedly pressing equals to generate the 3 times table. I asked, 'So can you do any table?' and he replied that you '... can do the 24 times table.'

Although I saw few incidents involving discoveries with computers, there was one respect in which some children appeared to be trying to explore using them. This was in attempting to exit from programs and move either to a different level or to a different program. However, adults generally discouraged this during lessons. There was a different approach, however, in the lower set when the children used the computers before school. At this time, they were allowed and expected to explore the computers. This often meant use of games but not always. On one occasion, I joined the children using computers before school. Three of the four computers were in use;

one was being used for games, one for area and one for fractions. I believe the children had chosen these programs themselves from those available. The teacher was enthusiastic about this informal use and believed it improved the children's computer skills and independent use of the computers. There was only one occasion when this informal use was mentioned in a maths lesson:

> The teacher was using shapes on an overhead projector to discuss equivalent fractions with the class. Many of the questions were unanswered. The teacher asked, 'How many tenths in a half?' Miriam gave the correct answer, five, without any help. The teacher asked her how she did it and Miriam replied, 'Well, I went to the computer and worked it out.' The teacher acknowledged that she had probably used a computer program related to this in the past.

Miriam's answer to the teacher's question was perplexing to start with. At the time the question was asked, she did not go to the computer, but she appeared to be referring to past use, probably informal use before school. This was a useful reminder that such use may have had a positive influence on the children's mathematics learning. The incident was particularly striking given that Miriam was one of the children considered to have most difficulty with mathematics and yet she answered this question when others in the room did not.

Discussion

Level of use

My findings are in line with other work pointing to a low level of calculator use in English schools in recent years (e.g. SCAA 1997; Ruthven 2001). The low level of use was roughly in keeping with the *Framework for Teaching Mathematics* (DfEE 1999a) though the ways schools used calculators did not necessarily match the detail of the framework. In particular, in one of the schools, it had been decided that Year 3 and 4 children would benefit from calculator use. The amount of use I saw among Year 5 children was lower than that observed by inspectors (OFSTED 2000). My findings about computer use are also in line with inspection findings (OFSTED 2001). This applies both to the relatively low level of use during mathematics lessons and the fact that the most common use was for consolidation of skills. This low level of use means that there is little point in speculating about the effect calculator or computer use had on these children's attainment. Instead, my analysis will focus on the detail of the lessons I observed and what insights they might offer about calculator use and, to a lesser extent, computer use.

Calculators for checking

Checking was the only calculator activity common to all the classes where calculators were used. This is in line with other findings. For example, SCAA (1997) reported that in some schools calculator use was restricted to the checking of calculations done by other means. My own interviews with teachers, prior to the current study, revealed that some of the teachers interviewed commonly viewed a calculator as a tool for checking (Houssart 2000). This is regarded as a low-level use by Rousham and Rowland (1996) who have doubts about it as an activity, suggesting that some children may question the point of doing the calculation by other methods first. My observations suggest that this activity did not work for all children simply because some children did not carry out the activity as suggested by the teacher. Neither Wesley nor Neil seemed prepared to carry out calculations by other means if they knew the next step was to do so with a calculator. Instead, they moved straight to calculator use, perhaps suggesting that they regarded this activity as pointless. However, there were children who reacted differently. For Linda, there did seem to be some point in checking her answer with a calculator because she had genuine doubt about whether the answer was right. Also of note are her words to me, 'Don't tell me,' as she embarked on the check herself. This was in marked contrast to Linda's usual behaviour, which was to seek adult help and reassurance at every possible point. The calculator seemed to give her another way of finding out and thus reduce her dependence on adults. Checking also helped Seth in a different way, in that he realised that he could do some calculations faster in his head than with a calculator.

Calculator difficulties

The children I was working with sometimes made mistakes in pressing keys and also became confused by things such as the M for memory appearing in the display. This supports the views expressed elsewhere (SCAA 1997) that children do not automatically pick up calculator use and would benefit from more direct instruction. Many of the children I observed had difficulties with decimal answers, a problem that has been observed by others (Shuard *et al.* 1991; Ruthven and Chaplin 1997). I also observed difficulties with simpler aspects of number, which give clues about how these children could be helped in other ways. A very common problem was with the operation keys, suggesting that children had difficulty matching the symbol to the word or the operation. The calculator also confirmed the problems some individuals had with reading numbers. This finding can be interpreted in different ways. One reading of the situation is that children who cannot reliably recognise symbols for operations or read numbers with two or three digits should not be using calculators. However, another approach would be to harness calculators to help children with these difficulties.

Discovering number properties

My observations also included positive aspects of calculator provision, similar to those reported by advocates of calculator use (Shuard *et al.* 1991; Rousham and Rowland 1996). There was also evidence of the role of the calculator in motivating and empowering children as suggested by Anghileri (2000). In particular, there was interest and excitement about the decimal answers obtained in the division investigation. In the same lesson, some children were also able to move towards a generalisation about what happens when you divide a number by itself. Sharing discoveries was an important part of this lesson, planned by the teacher. Sometimes comparing discoveries and results was an unofficial activity initiated by the children. For example, the discussion between Jed and Wesley led to fruitful discovery of the constant function and its use in generating tables. My observations suggest that many of the children were interested in and motivated by the things that happened when they used the calculators. The calculator has the potential to play a dual role in both arousing children's interest and presenting them with new aspects of number, such as recurring decimals.

Calculators and individuals

Although some of the children experienced difficulties in the calculator lessons, many of these were similar to difficulties shown elsewhere and were not caused by the calculator. This applies to Neil's difficulty in reading numbers; Claire's reluctance to acknowledge an answer did not make sense; and Erica's difficulty with the symbol for subtraction. Some children performed better than usual when calculators were available. In the case of Wesley and Lawrence, this seemed to be because they moved away from the procedures which they did not like using to being able to explore numbers and work things out for themselves. The case of Douglas is particularly interesting, bringing the maths fairy to mind. His teacher's enthusiasm for his explanation of the constant function reflects the fact that his behaviour in the calculator lesson was in marked contrast to that in other mathematics lessons. He was able to explain confidently something he had been taught the day before. In the same lesson I also observed him able to use what he had been taught to complete a task without reminder or encouragement. This was unusual behaviour for Douglas, who generally needed coaxing to do anything. It also meant the adults needed to reconsider the view that he could not remember anything and was unaware of what he was doing.

Use of computers

Due to the comparatively few opportunities I had for close observation of children using computers, it is difficult to draw any firm conclusions. Nevertheless, it is possible to make some observations, especially when points emerge similar to those already mentioned with regard to calculators. One striking similarity is that computers, like calculators, seem to suit some children. Douglas was the clearest example, responding positively to both computer and calculator use in comparison to other work. Seth, on the other hand, seemed to have difficulties in computer lessons, which were not apparent in other lessons. My informal discussions with children suggest that one factor was computer access at home with some of the most confident users, such as Quam Nam, being experienced at use of computers and of the Internet. Seth was not alone in his difficulties, though, and like calculators, computers presented many children with practical difficulties when it came to use of keyboards.

Classroom suggestions

Observing and listening

Observing and listening to children using calculators can provide insights about their understanding of number. In particular, classroom assistants, working alongside children using calculators, are likely to observe both their strengths and difficulties. Below is a list of the things adults might look and listen for when children use calculators:

- Can the children correctly identify the symbols on the operation keys?
- Can they correctly enter large numbers into the calculator?
- Can they read numbers from the display, including large numbers and decimals?
- Do they know how to correct a mistake made on the calculator?
- Are they experiencing distractions, for example when M or E appears in the display?
- Do they show an interest in or knowledge of other keys on the calculator, perhaps learned outside school?
- Are they showing an interest in unusual or unexpected answers and a willingness to discuss them further?
- Are they showing understanding of aspects not yet taught, such as decimals or negative numbers?

When children use computers, ask yourself:

- Are children ready to move on to a higher level for a given program or on to a different program?
- Do children have knowledge from computer use at home that can be exploited?
- Do children have difficulties using the computer keyboard, for example in identifying the letters?

Planning and teaching

The ideas below are again based on my observations and teachers may find some or all of them appropriate for the children they teach. Many of them are linked to suggestions made above:

- Some children may benefit from direct instruction about how to use calculators, perhaps using an overhead calculator.
- Some children may be able to share their knowledge about calculator use with the rest of the class.
- Help may be needed to overcome particular difficulties observed by the teacher or other adults, such as double pressing or distractions caused by the memory symbol.
- Calculators can present another way of teaching basic ideas such as how to read numbers from the display or matching symbols to operation keys.
- Children using calculators should be encouraged to discuss what they are doing and what answers they have obtained. This will

offer opportunities to relate language to symbols and to read numbers from the display.

- Children making discoveries on calculators should be encouraged to share them with the others.
- If issues such as large numbers, or negative numbers or decimals arise, it is worth using the opportunity to see if some children show some understanding of and interest in these ideas.
- Children may also need help to overcome difficulties with the computer keyboard. This may be in the form of adult support or in alternative ways of carrying out operations such as accessing websites.
- Some children may have computer expertise which they can share with others and which can be exploited in planning lessons. Children may be able to work at different levels of computer programs.

8 Easy tasks, hard tasks, elastic tasks

The teacher was introducing multiplication of two-digit numbers by single-digit numbers using vertical format. The first example on the blackboard was 14×1. The teacher went through this, multiplying first the 4 by 1 and the 1 by 1. I was sitting next to Matthew, who had a whispered conversation with me about 'One times anything' and arrived at the answer 14 in a single calculation. Matthew was asked to go to the board and do the second calculation, 14×2, which he did correctly. As he came back to his seat, he said, 'Pips, mate.'

Introduction

This chapter differs from earlier chapters in that it deals with tasks not according to the way they are presented, but according to their level of difficulty. In this chapter I will describe the reactions of various children to hard work and to easy work. I will also describe some children working on tasks which were differentiated in various ways, or open in order to allow differing responses. The main finding of this chapter is that making work easy and repetitive was counterproductive for many children. There were instances where performances declined as tasks became easier and instances where harder work engaged children. Although making the work harder sometimes had positive effects, there were also occasions when the work presented considerable difficulties for some children.

Background

Differing needs

Central to discussions about ease of work and selecting work for pupils is the idea that individual pupils have differing needs and in particular are likely to have different levels of attainment. This idea has had widespread support in English primary schools for many years. The Cockcroft Report, published in 1982, contained an oft-quoted paragraph about the 'seven year gap'. This gave an example of a place value activity which some 7-year-olds could answer correctly but some 14-year-olds could not (Cockcroft 1982: paragraph 342). The implication was that teachers could expect a seven-year spread of attainment within a year group. In primary schools, this often meant within one class. As Brown (1999) points out, this led to an emphasis on curricular differentiation. This often meant either allowing children to work through published material at their 'own pace' or grouping children by attainment and giving different work to the different groups.

Matching tasks to children

Research on tasks in British primary schools confirms that level of difficulty is a factor considered by teachers in task selection, but that there are problems in matching the level of difficulty to the children involved (Bennett *et al.* 1984). Level of difficulty is also considered a relevant factor in identifying children's mathematical errors (Cockburn 1999). Cockburn suggests that errors are likely to result from over-challenging tasks. She does not discuss the consequences of under-challenging tasks. Wiliam *et al.* (1999) report on interviews with bottom set pupils from secondary schools, many of whom raised this issue.

Curriculum for low attainers

Both the use of individualised schemes and, to a lesser extent, the use of ability grouping still mean that all pupils have access to broadly the same curriculum, though some pupils will meet certain parts of it later than others. Another possibility for children considered to have special needs is the alternative curriculum as outlined by Robbins (2000). He says that in special schools this often consisted of an individualised approach focusing on arithmetic. In mainstream schools it could mean withdrawal of children from mainstream classes for remedial work. In both cases the mathematical content was likely to be limited compared to that experienced by other children.

There are those who argue that it is not necessary to remove challenge from work designed for low attainers. For example, Trickett and Sulke (1988), building on the 'Low Attainers in Mathematics

Project' (1987), suggest that low attainers are able to cope with activities involving elements of mathematical challenge, including a temporary state of confusion or puzzlement. It is also sometimes suggested that rather than providing different tasks for children considered to have different levels of attainment, the same starting point can be used with all children but the eventual outcome will vary according to their response. Some examples of starting points of this type are given by Ollerton (2003) and are aimed at 7–16-year-olds.

Setting

If children are taught mathematics in sets, then the issue of the type of curriculum offered is raised. For example, the lower sets may be offered a broadly similar curriculum to other sets, but with some changes. Alternatives include working through the same content at a slower pace, removing some of the content, simplifying the tasks offered, or a combination of these. Another issue raised by setting is whether there is still a need to differentiate tasks within sets. Setting is seen by some as grouping children together with others with similar needs and attainment and hence removing most or all of the need for differentiation. Boaler (1997) suggests that the growth of setting in English schools in the 1990s reflected the focus on academic success. In considering the experiences of secondary pupils in different mathematics sets, Boaler *et al.* (2000) acknowledge work on the inequities of setting, with quantitative methods dominating. They point to the need to consider the effect of ability grouping on students' learning of mathematics, which might be done using qualitative methods including classroom observation. Such techniques have been used in other subjects. The results suggest that low-ability groups may be exposed to different curricular content (Oakes 1990) and experience poorer quality discussion (Gamoran 1993). Page (1989) found teachers of low-ability groups avoiding substantive debate.

Recent developments

As discussed in Chapter 1, contemporary advice is that as many children as possible should be included in the daily mathematics lesson. Too much individual planning is discouraged as is over-differentiating. This represents a change to recent practices in England which encouraged children to progress at their 'own pace'. This change can be seen as at least partly influenced by international comparisons that led to suggestions that countries where children were expected to progress together had higher standards of attainment.

The detail of the National Numeracy Strategy is organised according to the year group of the children and thus carries the assumption that children will be taught particular aspects of mathematics according to their age rather than level of attainment. The detail of the *Framework for Teaching Mathematics* (DfEE 1999a) is set out by year group and there is also an accompanying booklet offering examples of the standard expected of each year group (QCA 1999c). It is suggested in the framework that the needs of particular pupils can be met partly through differentiated group work, partly through open-ended tasks and partly through other teaching strategies. These strategies include questioning techniques such as starting with questions which all children can manage, targeting questions at particular pupils and using open questions. Other strategies include adapting materials for some pupils by using simplified vocabulary or offering resources such as number lines to support children.

In the classrooms

Three of the sets had marked similarities as far as level of difficulty was concerned. These sets all contained a small proportion of the year group and consisted only of children believed to have particular difficulty with mathematics. Most of the adults working with these sets had an interest in children with special needs and some had considerable experience in working with them. Thus the focus was in helping children who had learning difficulties in mathematics and sometimes other difficulties as well. The children in these sets were not expected to reach Level 4, the National Curriculum level officially expected of 11-year-olds, by the end of their primary schooling.

The lower set was in a different position. Although a few children with special needs were withdrawn for mathematics, this set consisted basically of what was considered to be the bottom half of the attainment range. Some children in the set were considered to have special needs as far as mathematics was concerned, but many were not. At this time, schools were under pressure to meet a nationally imposed target which said that at least 75 per cent of 11-year-olds should reach Level 4. If this school were to reach this target, then half the lower set would need to attain Level 4 by the end of primary school. This set followed work considered to be suitable for their year group according to the *Framework for Teaching Mathematics* and spent only the allocated time on each topic. The teacher of this set was a mathematics specialist and had taught a top set the previous year.

Easy work

There is a difficulty in defining easy work and in judging what is easy for a particular child. One criterion I adopted was that if children completed a piece of work in an extremely short time and apparently with little effort, then it could be said to be easy for them. There were occasions when this happened when at first glance it appeared an individual was not working at all. One example is the incident described here:

> The children were supposed to be completing a worksheet quietly, but Lawrence was out of his seat and whistling, which led to him being kept in at lunchtime. The worksheet in question was about multiplying single-digit numbers by two and required the children to put answers in boxes. Lawrence had started filling in answers while the sheets were given out and continued to do so while the teacher was explaining the work. It was only when the children were asked to start work that his disruptive behaviour started, but a glance at his worksheet while he was out of his seat confirmed that the sheet was completed.

Although most of the children were well behaved most of the time, there were a few other incidents similar to the one described above. This clearly suggests that the work was well within Lawrence's capability and raises questions about why he behaved in this way. It could have been a sign of boredom or dissent, or he could have hoped that this behaviour would draw attention to the fact that he had actually completed the task with ease.

Another possible indicator of easy work was comments from the children suggesting the work was easy. An example is given at the start of the chapter. In this case, Matthew said 'Pips, mate,' a phrase sometimes used by the children to indicate easy work. It is possible that Matthew carried out the calculation mentally or even knew the answer, whereas the teacher was trying to show the children how to carry out this calculation using a standard written method. Often, children did not seem to see the need for standard methods if they thought the calculations were easy enough to do by other means.

Getting easier

Sometimes I was able to judge that work was too easy for certain children because they had coped successfully with harder work on the same topic. Examples of this occurred during an extended block of work on fractions with the original Year 5 set. Sean, Wesley and Darren coped well with work at the beginning of the block. The teacher made the work easier as he was concerned that many of the children were not coping. I was able to chart the progress of the three boys as the work became easier. This set spent six weeks studying fractions. During this period, they were given eighteen worksheets that involved colouring in a given fraction, saying what fraction was coloured or labelling a section with the correct fraction. Although different fractions were dealt with in different weeks, there was little progression in the types of task on the worksheet. The response of these children to the fraction sheets is described in more detail elsewhere (Houssart 2002b). Here I will pick out a few incidents:

> It was the second week of studying fractions. The introductory part of the lesson was about how halves can be folded to give quarters. Wesley made a whispered intervention about whether thirds could be made in this way. Sean showed an interest in this idea but the teacher did not and the lesson moved on. The next part of the lesson involved completing a worksheet. As the sheets were given out, the children were reminded not to start until they had listened to the instructions. Sean did not abide by this but started work immediately and completed the sheet quickly without help.

Later on, I had the opportunity to look more closely at the children's worksheets. Sean had made a few small errors on this sheet, as had Wesley. None of the errors suggested mathematical misunderstanding, rather they suggested that the boys had not followed the instructions precisely. For example, one question consisted of shapes divided into two equal parts and asked the children to colour half red and half blue. Wesley did not use the colours stipulated and Sean wrote $\frac{1}{2}$ by each shape rather than colouring them. A few weeks later, I worked with Wesley and Darren during a lesson about eighths. By now, they were showing signs of boredom and not always completing their work correctly. The final week on fractions was about fifths and tenths:

The children were given a worksheet on fifths and tenths. For one question, they were given a circle divided into ten equal pieces and they had to colour each tenth a different colour. On the table where I was working, the focus was mainly on finding ten different coloured pencils. Sean was on a different table and I noticed he was working slowly or sometimes not at all, in marked contrast to the speed with which he tackled the fractions work in the first few weeks. In the discussion at the end of the lesson, the teacher asked, 'How many tenths make a fifth?' Someone answered, 'Two.' The teacher asked why and Sean replied, 'Because two fives make ten.'

When I looked at the folders, I found that Sean had not completed the sheet, stopping at the question which required ten different colours. The sheet was easier mathematically than the oral questions Sean had answered correctly. Compared with work done in previous weeks, the sheet could be seen as easier and was certainly no harder, though it did deal with different fractions. The teacher had been concerned about the difficulty children had with fractions and had therefore tried to make the work simple and fairly repetitive. For Wesley, Sean and Darren, this backfired and their written work became worse rather than better.

Getting harder

Work sometimes got harder when the teacher moved on to the next step. Sometimes it could be seen as getting harder because the work was presented in a more complex or unusual way. This caused anxiety in some children and led them to assume that they could not possibly do the work. However, there were some children who reacted positively when such work was introduced. An example was Penny, who did not always co-operate in mathematics lessons. There were several occasions, however, when the work became more difficult and Penny joined in:

> The children had been classifying 2D shapes according to the number of sides. For the first time the teacher included concave quadrilaterals in the selection of shapes presented. Penny's hand went up immediately the teacher started asking questions; she was clearly curious about these new shapes which were, as she put it, 'bent in'.

Penny's negative behaviour at the beginning of this lesson was probably not task-related. Penny sometimes came to a lesson apparently not in a mood to co-operate, possibly following incidents at playtime which preceded the lesson. Despite her original hostility, in all such cases she did eventually opt back in to the mathematics lesson. Another child who sometimes came to lessons in a negative mood was Craig. Like Penny, Craig ultimately opted back in to the lesson. The incident here occurred about six weeks after Craig joined the bottom set from a higher set. On this day he had not appeared for maths at the start of the lesson, but was later found, brought in by the head of year and asked to sit at the table where I was working with Penny:

> Craig sat with his arms folded and his back to the teacher and seemed not to listen as the task was explained. Penny made some comments to me about the task and although they were neither to Craig nor about him, he responded each time by saying 'So?' in an aggressive way. My attempts to encourage Craig to start work failed. Meanwhile Penny encountered difficulties with the task. It was presented in the form of a puzzle, but involved addition of two-digit numbers in horizontal format. Penny had done $35 + 19 + 36$ and arrived at the answer 720. She stood by her answer, despite my questioning, so she explained her method. She had added the tens getting 7 which she had written down first, then added the units getting 20. We talked about this and I helped her to adapt her method to get the correct answer. By the end of the discussion Craig was openly listening and gave his assent to the final answer. I suggested that he write the answer on his sheet and Penny invited him to come round to our side of the table so we could work together. He did so and we discussed ways of doing the next calculation.

Although I believe it was the task that encouraged Craig to join in, it could also be argued that my presence had an influence. In my assumed role I did try to encourage children to participate, as did the classroom assistants I worked alongside. The crucial point in the incident above is that not all forms of intervention worked. This was the first time I had worked near Craig, hence I had not built up a relationship with him and my initial attempts to get him to participate failed. My action in discussing an apparent mathematical contradiction with Penny was aimed at assisting her rather than interesting Craig, yet it seemed to achieve both ends.

Hard work

In the incidents described above, particular tasks were provided that were harder than usual. However, in the lower set, the work could almost always be seen as hard for the group of children I was particularly interested in. The word 'hard' can be taken to mean many things in this context. First, many of the lessons involved the children in using new techniques which had just been explained and which they did not seem to have fully understood at the point when they were asked to start work. Second, the children seemed to have problems with the component parts of each technique. For example, they did not seem to remember their number bonds or techniques for adding multiples of ten. In addition to this, there were often minor practical difficulties, such as copying from the board and drawing charts and diagrams correctly. One such lesson involved multiplication of two-digit by single-digit numbers. This lesson involved the grid diagrams described in Chapter 6:

> The teacher wrote five questions on the board, which involved multiplying two-digit numbers by single-digit numbers. He did the first one for them on the board using the grid method. The group I was working with returned to their places. First, they had to write the date and the title, 'Multiplication'. This was a distraction, especially for Miriam, who was concerned to write the date in a different form to the teacher, using dots between the numbers rather than dashes. Copying the first grid from the board took a long time. The teacher had not written the answers to the calculation in the grid, although they were by the side of it. This caused some confusion. Sarah did a grid six squares high and six squares wide, using the centimetre squares in her book. She was then worried that she would not be able to write the calculations on the right-hand side of the grid in the same way that the teacher had. The second calculation was 42×8. The first stage was to work out 40×8. Sarah did not seem to have a method for doing this, so I tried to remind her of the method the teacher had taught earlier, starting with 4×8. However, she did not have a method of working out 4×8, so we built it up from scratch, starting at 1×8. I moved on to see how Miriam was doing. She was trying to work out 30×6, presumably not realising that the teacher had written this on the board, though not in the box where she expected to see it. Meanwhile, Tony had moved on to the next calculation, which was 42×8. With a little

help, he arrived at the correct partial answers of 320 and 16. Unfortunately, when he wrote these down to add them up, he positioned the 16 incorrectly and arrived at the incorrect answer of 480.

Miriam's jottings for 30×6 are shown in Figure 8.1. She wrote the number 6 down 30 times. After that, she drew a line after the first twelve sixes. Underneath, she correctly wrote $12 \times 6 = 72$. I don't know how she arrived at this, but I do know that on other occasions she had looked up tables facts which the children had in their maths books. She had also identified that she now had to do 18×6. However, she did not get any further and drew a line under the calculation at this point, perhaps indicating that she was going to leave it there, though it is possible that at this point she realised they had already been given the answer. It is interesting to compare Miriam's attempt to do this on paper with her response during the introduction. When the teacher had broken up a calculation into parts and asked for the answer to 20×4, she was one of the fastest to give the correct answer. She appeared at the time to be following the method suggested by the teacher of linking 20×4 to 2×4. It is possible, however, that she was actually using a different method in her head, a method that she could not implement for 30×6.

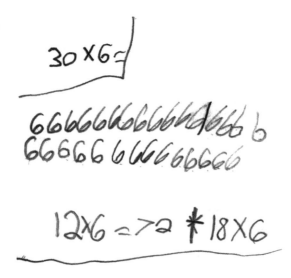

Figure 8.1 Miriam's jottings for 30×6

This was a very difficult lesson for this group of children and shows what can happen if several difficulties come together. It seems unlikely that they understood the method and the logic behind it. On top of this, they had difficulty in carrying out the individual multiplications, even when the calculation was broken down for them. They appeared to have forgotten how to multiply by multiples of 10 and they made errors in the column addition. There were also difficulties involved in copying from the board, drawing grids, writing the date and writing the title.

Responses to hard work

There were other occasions when the same group of children experienced great difficulties with the lesson. I became interested in how they responded to these difficulties. The observations below were made at the end of a lesson based on empty number lines, which was described in Chapter 4. The early part of this lesson presented many problems:

> Slowly the children seemed to pick up what they were supposed to do. Sarah, for example, was proud of doing a question on her own. When I looked at the question, she had used the right technique but reached the wrong answer because she thought you had to count on 40 to get from 30 to 50. While I was busy working with Sarah, Miriam and Heidi started working together. A bit later they told me they had done this and said if they didn't have help tomorrow, they would help each other.

> Near the end of the lesson, the teacher stopped the class and gave the answers to the five questions the children had been set. Tony asked for my help to complete the last one at this point and did so. This meant Tony did all five questions. Miriam, Heidi and Sarah did three and Damian did two. At the end of the lesson Tony told me he would keep his jottings so he would know what to do tomorrow.

It took an enormous effort for the children I worked with to complete a few examples in a lesson. Despite this, some positive things emerged. The first was that at the end of the lesson they did appear just able to do something they could not previously do. Sarah showed pride in her achievement, and in subsequent weeks she often reacted in a similar way, proudly showing me her book and saying things like 'I got them right', even if she had only done a few questions. Other positive aspects of this lesson were that Tony, Miriam and Heidi showed signs of developing strategies to 'help themselves'.

Elastic tasks

Occasionally, tasks were set that could be seen as 'elastic' in that the children could respond at different levels or could extend the task if appropriate. Some examples of such tasks have been described in earlier chapters, in particular some of the practical tasks discussed in Chapter 5 enabled the children to respond in different ways. I also observed elastic, oral and mental tasks. One example was the game 'Ladders'.

Ladders became an established game in the Year 4 class. When it was played, it was related to the table that the children had practised at the beginning of the lesson. Often, the children asked if they could play Ladders before starting the main part of the lesson. The game was played by one child coming to the front and walking along an imaginary ladder. The rest of the class had to say what number the child was on when they finished. The following example is drawn from the week when the lesson had started with the children reciting the 7 times table, which was written on the board. By now, the children knew the rules of Ladders. In this case, it meant that the children were to imagine a ladder going up in sevens. The chosen child would say which multiple of 7 they were starting on. They would then take slow, deliberate steps either forwards or backwards and the rest of the class would be asked which number they finished on.

> The teacher said they could play Ladders and Sarah was chosen to go first. She announced her starting number as 7. She took a step forward and paused. She did this fairly slowly three more times. Then she raised her hand, the signal that she had finished. The others correctly said that she was on 35.

> A bit later, Miriam was chosen to have a turn. She started on 21 and took four steps forward. She then took three steps backward. The other children correctly said she was on 28.

Sarah seemed to interpret the task in as simple a way as possible, starting at 7 and moving only forwards. Miriam complicated the task slightly by starting at a higher number and by including backward steps. However, the fact that all her forward steps were together and all her backward steps were together still kept the task relatively simple. Some children made the task far more complicated by starting on higher numbers and using combinations of forward and backward steps. It was interesting that on the whole pupils seemed to adapt this task to suit them and that the rest of the children seemed to accept the task at whatever level. As the year progressed, children tended to get more adventurous. They also adopted certain strategies, for example, some seemed to realise that you could take one forward step followed by one backward step and it did not change your position. This was sometimes done in the middle of a turn to make the move look complicated.

Differentiating oral tasks

Sometimes the teachers differentiated oral tasks by asking questions at different levels and targeting them at different children. One way of doing this was to start with easy questions and progress to more challenging ones. A slightly different way was to save challenging questions for a session at the end of the lesson. Some children, such as Sean and Wesley, seemed to look forward to and recognise such questions. Others, such as Julie, also seemed to recognise that hard questions were being asked and took no part in these sessions. Similarly, when work got progressively harder, some children would turn off at a certain point. A different strategy was to mix the level of difficulty of the questions:

> The teacher started asking questions about time. The first question was about how many minutes in an hour. He then asked other questions, including how many years in a millennium and how many days in a week. I noticed that Sarah had her hand up for some of the easier questions, like the number of days in a week. Miriam put her hand up when the teacher asked how many months in a year. She was chosen to answer but incorrectly answered 25. Later, the discussion moved on to days in a year and days in a leap year.

Several months later, the same children were discussing various units of measurement, including measurement of time. The teacher again used a mixture of questions:

> After talking about days in a year and in a leap year, the teacher asked why there was an extra day. No one answered, although

he said they had covered this before. The teacher explained about a year really consisting of 365¼ days. He moved on to talk about days in various months and then returned to ask why there was an extra day in a leap year. Miriam was the only person who had her hand up and although she had some difficulty in choosing her words she basically gave a correct answer.

Both these incidents suggest that some children appeared to listen throughout the session when a mixture of easy and hard questions was used. Often, their responses were predictable. For example, Sarah frequently put her hand up when easy questions were asked. There were some exceptions to this predictability. Miriam was wrong about the number of months in a year, even though it was a relatively easy question and she had chosen to answer it. On the other hand, in a later lesson, she succeeded with a difficult question about leap years that no one else in the class was prepared to answer. Both these sessions involved a mix of easy and hard questions in no apparent order. In one session, however, the teacher deliberately moved from easy to hard and back again:

The teacher wrote the number 16340 on the board and asked if anyone could read it. One child correctly answered, 'Sixteen thousand, three hundred and forty.' The teacher then added an extra digit at the beginning of the number, making it 416340. This was harder for the children to read, so the teacher helped by labelling the units, tens, hundreds, and so on. When the correct answer had been established, he added an extra digit, making the new number 5416340. Next time round, the teacher started with a four-digit number and added digits in the same way. After this, he wrote a three-digit number on the board, which was 207. He reminded children that every hand should be up in the early stages. Miriam put her hand up and correctly read the number. A digit was added to make the number 4207 and Heidi was asked to read this but didn't answer. Several moves on, Damian correctly read the number 24764207. The teacher congratulated him on this and moved on to give the final example, which caused some excitement. This was 324764207.

This incident suggests that the teacher was trying hard to use a range of numbers so that everyone could answer at least some of the questions. The fact that he moved from small to large numbers then back again prevented children from switching off as they sometimes did when teachers concentrated on either easy or hard questions for a reasonable period of time. However, the way the questions gradually got harder also performed an important mathematical function in that the children were able to build up each number starting from its smaller components. In this way, many of the children with difficulties were able to succeed on the harder questions. The murmur of excitement that greeted the last number was also interesting in that it implied a preference for challenging examples.

Discussion

Opting out

The issue of opting out was discussed in an earlier chapter where it was suggested that a few children opted out of tasks that were presented in a way that did not suit them. In this chapter, we have seen that a few children opted out of tasks because the level of difficulty was inappropriate for the child. Perhaps surprisingly, the majority of incidents concerned tasks which were too easy. There were three main reasons for suggesting that the tasks were too easy. The first concerned 'fake opting-out' when the task was actually completed very quickly, as in the example given earlier of Lawrence and the worksheet. The second was by comparison with harder tasks on the same topic which children had completed successfully. This occurred during the block of work on fractions. The third was because children sometimes opted back in when a harder task was presented.

Although there were several incidents of opting out and opting back, they occurred relatively rarely and were confined to a small number of children, most of whom had a history of potentially challenging behaviour. Most of the children, most of the time, did not refuse so publicly to do the tasks set. However, closer observation suggested that the relatively small number of opting out or back incidents were supported by a larger number of incidents where problems were caused by the level of difficulty of the task. Many children appeared less motivated when the work got easier, although a few reacted when it got harder.

The main mathematical issue raised is the way many children preferred more challenging tasks. Sometimes it was just a case of the task getting harder, on others it was making it less routine or repetitive. Sometimes, as in the story of Penny and the concave shapes, an element of surprise engaged children. At other times, as with Craig and the addition task, it was an apparent contradiction that attracted their interest. In this respect my findings are in line with those of others (Low Attainers in Mathematics Project 1987; Trickett and Sulke 1988), who suggest that low-attaining students can cope with activities involving elements of mathematical challenge.

Hard work

Although the appearance of hard work often had positive consequences, this was not always the case. Problems with hard work particularly arose in the lower set where the teacher was following both the content and pace advised for children of a given age in the *Framework for Teaching Mathematics* (DfEE 1999a). Although this was not always problematic, there were some extreme examples of work which appeared far too hard for some of the children. My initial reaction to this was of sympathy with the children as they seemed to lack the skills required and I was doubtful whether they understood. I expected the situation to worsen as the year progressed. However, this was not the case. What seemed to happen instead was that the children developed strategies to cope with their difficulties as described in the number line lesson. Often children were aware that they managed to do things they initially could not do. They saw this as positive and seemed less inclined to compare themselves with others in the class who usually did more questions and had less difficulty. Over the year, this group of children continued to work in a similar way, usually working very hard to complete a few questions. There were exceptions, though. For example, there was one week when Sarah correctly completed all the work given and was given an extension sheet. My original fear that the children would get more behind and become more confused was not realised. Instead, they found ways of coping and kept up with the work, though only just. As I got to know the set better, I also realised that difficulties were not confined to the small group I knew best. Many of the other children, even some of those regarded as the highest attainers, had occasional difficulties. This was evident in the number line lesson, where the teacher felt the need to re-explain the activity to the whole class. Thus, although it was sometimes possible to predict who would find the work easy and who would find it difficult, this was not always the case.

Elastic tasks

Although there were comparatively few tasks which children could respond to at different levels, these tasks often had interesting outcomes. For example, when playing Ladders, the children almost always came up with examples at an appropriate level. Similarly, when asked to investigate symmetry of shapes, children worked at a level which they seemed to understand. It is interesting to compare responses to these tasks to Douglas's work with the computer described in the last chapter. In this case, Douglas had wanted to work at a higher level but had made an inappropriate choice in trying to go straight to the hardest level. I did not see enough examples of children being able to fix their own level of work to draw any firm conclusions. However, I would tentatively suggest that giving them scope to choose examples or respond in different ways to a task was more successful than a stark choice of levels.

Classroom suggestions

Observing and listening

Those working alongside children should have opportunities to notice how they respond to changes of difficulty in work or to periods of similar work. Here are things to look and listen for:

- Do some children switch off when harder questions are asked, perhaps at the end of a lesson?
- Do some children show a particular interest in extension questions but less enthusiasm for simple and repetitive questions?
- If similar work is repeated over a period of time, which children gain in confidence and enthusiasm for the work? Do any children react negatively and show a decline in performance?
- Do some children have frequent difficulty when new work is introduced and need the component parts of the work to be explained?

Planning and teaching

As with many other issues, there does not seem to be a strategy which works for all children. However, there are some things that teachers may wish to try:

- Include a mixture of levels of difficulty in oral sessions, perhaps sometimes moving in and out of difficult tasks.
- Consider sometimes targeting tasks at particular children but sometimes offering opportunities for others to answer.

- Try to include some tasks which children can respond to at a variety of levels and where they have some say in determining the level they work at.
- Beware of assuming that simply repeating simple work will lead to mastery of the work. Sometimes it may be better to accept partial success and move on to something else.
- When children are introduced to a new task, they may need help in remembering how to carry out the component parts of the task.

9　Assessment tasks

At the start of the lesson, the teacher gave out two sheets about fractions. One of these was a straightforward sheet requiring children to
colour in fifths and tenths. The other sheet was harder and involved
equivalence, something which had been mentioned in extension work
at various points in the block but not formally taught. The teacher
appeared to make a last-minute decision not to cover the work on
equivalence. He told the children not to do the equivalence sheet but
went through the easier sheet in detail before asking the children to
complete it. Darren and Wesley started to do the equivalence sheet
instead of the colouring sheet. When the teacher discovered this, he
said, 'If this was your test, you've failed.' Some weeks later, I found
the equivalence sheet in Wesley's folder. It was mostly correct.

Introduction

A range of assessment tasks were used in all the sets and this is
reflected in this chapter. The first incidents used illustrate how assessment sometimes arose from teaching but became explicit, especially if
several adults were present. Following this, planned assessment tasks
are considered, which include individual assessment, written tasks,
short tests and more formal tests. The chapter suggests that some
forms of assessment, usually the less formal, could give some insights
into children's strengths and difficulties. However, all forms of
assessment presented problems of some type and there were few, if
any, occasions when it could be said with confidence that the assessment had provided a true picture. This raises the question about
whether it is reasonable to say that a child can or cannot do something or whether we should restrict ourselves to saying that they did
something successfully on a particular occasion and in certain
circumstances.

Background

Approaches to assessment

Assessment takes many forms and can be categorised in various ways. For example, Black (1999) talks about summative assessment used to inform judgements about overall achievement and formative assessment, concerned with the short-term collection of evidence for guidance in learning. He goes on to discuss formative practice in classrooms in the UK at the time of writing. He raises concern about the negative impact of some forms of assessment due to the fact that marking and grading functions are over-emphasised and the giving of advice and the learning function are under-emphasised. He also says that pupils are compared with each other rather than assessment being concerned with personal improvement. This is likely to have a negative impact on pupils who perform poorly compared with others. Although formative assessment can take the form of marking and testing, there is also an element of informal teacher judgements made as part of everyday teaching. However, Watson (2001) says that even these judgements cannot be totally free of bias. She questions the assumption that it is possible to find out what a learner knows. She also points out that when teachers make informal judgements, they are inevitably involved in selection and interpretation. In doing this, they are influenced by their views about the pupil concerned and about mathematics.

Assessment systems inevitably influence the curriculum and approaches to teaching. Black (1998) suggests that high-stakes testing constrains both teachers and pupils to align their learning to meet the demands of tests. He also talks about problems of reliability and validity, particularly in the context of formal testing. He outlines many problems, some of which have been extensively researched. He also talks briefly about the fact that any one pupil might perform differently on different days. He says this problem appears to have received less attention in terms of research than other issues of reliability and validity.

External tests and targets

At the time this research was carried out, external tests for 11-year-olds and their associated targets were a very high-profile issue. In addition to these compulsory tests, the QCA had developed standardised tests in mathematics to be used with children at the end of Years 3, 4 and 5. The stated purpose of these tests is to support schools in monitoring children's progress. The tests are accompanied by teachers' guides (e.g. QCA 1998b). As well as containing answers and marking schemes, these booklets contain tables of age-standardised scores, national comparisons and information about interpreting the outcomes of the tests. A section on special needs suggests which children the tests are aimed at. For example, the Year 5 tests are designed to be used with children working at Levels 3–5. This section also discusses the assistance teachers can give to help children with particular needs, such as reading difficulties or lack of fluency in English.

The National Numeracy Strategy

The *National Numeracy Strategy: Framework for Teaching Mathematics* (DfEE 1999a) says that assessment recording and reporting are important elements of teaching. It goes on to classify assessments into three sections: short-term, medium-term and long-term. Short-term assessments are said to be an informal part of every lesson which enable teachers to check that children have grasped the main points in a lesson, to identify any misunderstandings and to check that they are remembering number facts. It is suggested that information from short-term assessments may be used to brief support staff about which children to assist and how to assist them. Medium-term assessment is said to be mainly about reviewing and recording progress in relation to key objectives. In some cases, medium-term assessments can link to individual education plans and can also help teachers to see whether any weaknesses remain. The section about long-term assessments deals mainly with end-of-year assessments. It talks of pupils' progress assessed in the light of school and national targets and the key objectives for the year.

The role of learning support assistants

At the time of my research there had been an increase in the number of assistants working alongside teachers, particularly with children considered to have special needs. A recent research report (Farell *et al.* 1999) suggests that for some assistants, aspects of assessment are part of their role. For example, it says that although monitoring and writing reports were seen as the job of teachers, many assistants were involved in this process and felt that their views were considered. Some made written or verbal contributions to reviews or reports.

Other sources suggest classroom assistants are likely to have an important role in informal classroom assessment as they are likely to hear and see things of importance. For example, in a handbook for classroom assistants (Aplin 1998), a section is devoted to the importance of listening to children. This book also suggests that by listening to children, assistants will gain important assessment information. In the short section of the book addressed to teachers, it is suggested that assistants can provide them with valuable information. Similar points are made by Fox (1998) who says that an assistant working closely with a particular pupil or group is likely to be more sensitive to their needs and reactions in any given situation than the class teacher. She goes on to say that it is important that assistants are able to give feedback to teachers.

In the classrooms

Like all teachers, those I worked with made judgements about the children's mathematics as part of their everyday teaching. The fact that there were extra adults in the classrooms meant that sometimes teachers shared these judgements. In one class in particular, the other adults were encouraged to participate in this day-to-day assessment. Slightly more formal assessment took various forms. In all the sets, pieces of written work had their place in assessment, both informally and formally. Short tests were also used in some of the sets.

Because none of the children I worked with were at the end of Key Stage 2, statutory assessment was not carried out. However, both schools had started to use the QCA optional tests for all year groups towards the end of the year. The two schools had different policies about using these tests with children who appeared to have learning difficulties. In one of the schools, all children were expected to take the tests, regardless of their level of attainment. In the other school, the adults could use their discretion in exempting children for whom they thought the tests were not appropriate.

Assessment during teaching

In one of the classrooms, discussions sometimes arose between the adults in the room about children's responses to tasks. Such tasks formed part of the normal teaching and were not planned as assessment tasks. Discussion often arose when children experienced difficulties:

The children were sitting on the mat and working on counting activities. One activity involved 2p coins being dropped in a glass jar. The children had to close their eyes and count in twos in their heads, using the sound of the coins dropping in the jar. When 12p was dropped in the jar, Neil said it was 22p and Claire said 10p. Most others seemed to get the correct answer.

The next example was 20p. Only three hands went up at the end, two of them offering the correct answer. The next example was 14p. Several incorrect answers were offered, for example 12, 16, 22, 31. The next example was 18p and this again led to several incorrect answers.

At this point the teacher and the support assistant started to discuss the activity. They seemed surprised at the difficulty the children had with this compared to similar activities. They talked about the fact that the children did better with numbers up to 10 and concluded that they needed to concentrate on counting in twos between 10 and 20 in future activities.

The end of the discussion between the two adults suggests that they were trying to work out on the spot what it might be about the activity that proved difficult for the children. Similar short discussions occurred on other occasions. Explanations for difficulties were not always forthcoming. One week the teacher admitted to being 'mystified' when the children appeared to have difficulty with a counting activity which they had managed on other occasions. Sometimes most of the children seemed to have difficulty with an activity. On other occasions, the difficulty was confined to one or two individuals:

The teacher was leading an activity using a large hundred square and a plastic spider which she moved around the square. At one point the spider was on 64. The teacher said that his dinner was on '20 more' and the children had to say which number this was. Douglas was asked but said he was not sure and didn't give a number. Other children then answered correctly. The activity continued with different examples and one of the support assistants helped Douglas, who was sitting near her. A little later she told the teacher that she thought Douglas was 'struggling' and asked if he could move nearer to the hundred square so he could touch it. The teacher initially agreed, but then had the idea of giving Douglas a smaller hundred square to work with. She handed the hundred square to the support assistant, who worked with Douglas on the next examples using it. Neil, who was sitting nearby, also made some use of it.

Looking back at this incident, I wonder whether the support assistant started watching Douglas when he didn't give an answer to the teacher's earlier question. Because her intervention was made immediately, Douglas was given something to help him with subsequent examples; raising the matter afterwards would not have had this effect. After further help and encouragement from the assistant, Douglas was able to answer the questions correctly. Provision of the hundred square was also of help to Neil. This suggests that what appears to be a difficulty confined to one child may be more widespread. This incident also suggests shared values between the teacher and assistant in wanting to help the children understand the mathematics, rather than just giving the correct answer.

Individual assessment

In the special needs set, learning support assistants were sometimes asked to assess individuals on work recently covered, using a list of items provided by the teacher. On one occasion I was asked to assess some children in this way. One of the items included was addition of numbers with totals up to 10. The first child I worked with was Damian:

> I asked Damian to add some pairs of single-digit numbers. He knew the answer to $5 + 5$ and used his fingers for the others. He then said he could do some others and asked to write on my pad. He wrote the addition $700 + 400$ in vertical format, then filled in the correct answer and was able to read it. We moved on to the next item on my list, which was addition of three single-digit numbers. Damian appeared to have difficulty in remembering the numbers, so I suggested he wrote them down. He wrote $3 + 4 + 2$ and arrived at the correct answer of 9 after a few attempts. He then said, 'I can also do ...' and wrote $100 + 217$ in vertical format. He worked from left to right filling in the answer 417. I asked him to check $1 + 2$ and he did so but still made it 4.

Working with Damian in this way raised an issue that almost always occurred during individual assessments. This was the issue of how accurate and consistent the children had to be before I could tell the teacher they could do the item or before I ticked a box on the sheet I had been given. Almost always, children could do some but not all of the examples given. The incident above was also of interest for Damian's own contribution. He seemed keen to show me that he could add three-digit numbers in vertical format. As far as I was aware, he had only been taught to add single-digit numbers at school so I wondered whether he had worked with larger numbers at home. Although he carried out the first addition correctly, the method used would not work with all numbers and he had also chosen relatively easy numbers. On the basis of this one calculation, it would probably not be reasonable to say that Damian could add three-digit numbers, but it was certainly true that he could sometimes do so, given suitable examples. Something similar could be said about adding single-digit numbers. Although he was correct with $5 + 5$, he needed fingers for other calculations and needed written reminders and several attempts when given three numbers. Finally, he made a mistake with the apparently simple calculation of $1 + 2$ when carrying it out in columns. Our discussion suggests that he was answering the calculation $1 + 2$ with 4, though it is possible that he was actually adding one more, having misremembered a rule about carrying.

Discussion with other adults confirmed that they often came across uneven performance when assessing individuals. Sometimes we could be more confident that children were able to do something and on other occasions they had apparent difficulties. This often led to discussion among the adults after the lesson:

> Towards the end of the Spring term, Mrs Taylor had been asked by the teacher to carry out assessments of individuals against a list of items. At the end of the lesson Mrs Taylor told us that Douglas had appeared to have great difficulty with the items, for example, failing to tell her the number after 88. The rest of us talked about things we had seen Douglas do on that day and other days. This led to speculation about why some of the children performed inconsistently. We also talked about whether it is fair to base assessment on performance on a particular day, especially if it contradicts observations made on other days.

In our discussion we tried to explain why Douglas had not been able to carry out the assessment task. Our discussion confirmed that he had difficulties with other tasks that day. Comparing these incidents led us to conclude that Douglas was having a difficult day and it would not be fair to take today's performance as an indication of what he could do. Possibly, factors outside school contributed to this. We speculated about whether the fact that it was the end of term and a holiday was due meant that Douglas was tired and not at his best. It is also possible that there were other reasons why Douglas did not perform well on those tasks. He had reacted much more positively the previous week when he had shown me a computer task, as described in an earlier chapter.

Written tasks

The children's written work contributed to their assessment in a fairly general way. Teachers looked regularly at written work to help them gauge the children's progress and they occasionally looked back through children's books or looked at collections of work in folders. Sometimes, written tasks served a more specific assessment function when a particular piece of work was used by teachers to form judgements. Usually, when this happened, the children were given less adult help than usual with the task and sometimes the task was given at the start of the lesson with little or no instruction or explanation.

Occasionally written tasks were used for assessment purposes some time after children had carried out the work concerned. On one day when I was not present, the children in the original Year 5 set were given a written sheet about multiplying by 4 which required them to put in missing numbers. These sheets were stored with all the fraction sheets in the children's folders:

> I looked at the sheet in Sean's folder. He had 29 questions right, 7 wrong and had not done the last 4. At the bottom of the sheet the teacher had written, 'Sean doesn't fully know his tables. This surprises me. More work needed.'

A copy of the sheet containing Sean's answers is shown in Figure 9.1. A closer look at this sheet shows that although Sean answered some questions incorrectly, many of these had already been answered correctly, albeit in a slightly different form, elsewhere on the same sheet. It is possible that Sean was confused by questions being repeated, though sometimes he did give the same answer to repeated questions. Possibly Sean lost concentration or ran out of time as the sheet progressed. He got the first ten questions right, but performed increasingly poorly in later sections.

In this case, as well as the worksheet performing an assessment function, the folders containing the sheets were also used for similar

×4 tables

2 × 4 = 8 ✓	4 × 10 = 16 ✗	4 × 6 = 26 ✗	4 × 4 = 16 ✓
6 × 4 = 24 ✓	6 × 4 = 24 ✓	1 × 4 = 4 ✓	4 × 8 = 16 ✗
8 × 4 = 32 ✓	4 × 4 = 16 ✓	6 × 4 = 24 ✓	7 × 4 = 28 ✓
3 × 4 = 12 ✓	2 × 4 = 8 ✓	9 × 4 = 36 ✓	0 × 4 = 0 ✓
7 × 4 = 28 ✓	0 × 4 = 0 ✓	10 × 10 = 40 ✗	4 × 4 = 4 ✗
1 × 4 = 4 ✓	1 × 4 = 4 ✓	5 × 4 = 20 ✓	9 × 4 = 32 ✗
0 × 4 = 0 ✓	3 × 4 = 12 ✓	3 × 4 = 12 ✓	4 × 9 = _
4 × 4 = 16 ✓	10 × 4 = 40 ✓	0 × 4 = 0 ✓	_ × 4 = 24
7 × 4 = 28 ✓	7 × 4 = 28 ✓	5 × 4 = 20 ✓	3 × _ = 12
10 × 4 = 40 ✓	9 × 4 = 36 ✓	4 × 2 = 16 ✗	_ × _ = 16

Figure 9.1 Sean's multiplication sheet

purposes. The folders of work had been collected together to make them available for a forthcoming inspection as well as for other purposes. The teacher had allowed me to look at the folders of the group of children I had been sitting with that term. This group included Darren, but his folder was nowhere to be found. Darren had told me about his lost folder in a previous lesson and I had helped him to look for it. Other adults had done the same but it never turned up. Thus the use of a folder of work as a contribution to assessment was meaningless in the case of Darren, who had no folder.

Classroom tests

Three of the four sets had fairly regular short written tests as part of their work. Some issues arising from the tests have already been discussed in Chapter 3. Some more examples are included below. The first incident took place very early in the term and during my first visit to the classroom. I was sitting next to Matthew and Bryn, Adrian and Nadeem were working on the same table:

The first question was to add 5 and 7. I noticed that Matthew did this by drawing first five circles then seven circles. He got the answer right. A later question was 12 + 6 and Matthew asked, 'Can we use fingers?' His question was not answered but he got this one right too. Question 8 on the test was '10 + 10 + 10'. Matthew muttered that he couldn't do this, though he eventually wrote the incorrect answer of 19. The next question was, 'Write thirty-seven in numbers or figures.' Again, Matthew said he couldn't do this and he left it blank. At the end of the test, the children marked their own answers. Matthew got 8 out of 10 with the two questions just mentioned being the ones he got wrong. The other three boys on the table all got 10 out of 10.

Two weeks later, I was sitting with the same group of children when they had another mental arithmetic test. This time, Matthew behaved differently during the test. Although I was sitting next to him, he had his arms round the paper so that neither I nor the other boys could see his answers. He made no comment on the questions, though sometimes I could see how he was working them out. For example, he used a ruler for one of the additions. At the end, having marked his own, Matthew got 10 out of 10. Although Matthew had certainly been trying to get the questions right the first time, I did wonder if he had changed a few of the answers, though I could not be sure of this. Much later in the year, the children had their final mental arithmetic test. I was sitting with Penny.

There were twenty questions in the test. Penny worked slowly and with apparent care, sometimes working things out at the bottom of the paper. Often she got behind because she was still working out the last answer when another question was asked. I was able to see a few of Penny's answers, though I was mostly concentrating on writing down the questions myself. One question asked how many tens in 170 and I realised I was uncertain what answer the teacher expected. I saw Penny write the answer 7, though later the answer was given as 17. Penny made a mistake on the question that asked how many toes there were in the class, given that nineteen children were present. Like many others, she appeared to count round the room for this one, and arrived at the incorrect answer of 170. I also noticed that when asked the mathematical name for a tennis ball, she wrote 'cylinder'. Despite all this, when the answers were marked, Penny got 20 out of 20. At the end, children had to put their hands up according to the mark they got. The number of hands up for full-marks, compared with the apparent confusion in the room at some points, made me wonder if others had done the same.

This was the only occasion when I was certain that answers had been changed in a test, though there were other times when I thought it a possibility. Whatever Penny's motive, it did not seem to be avoiding doing the mathematics. She worked determinedly on every question and seemed to go to great lengths to get the answers. I don't know if, while she was doing this, she was aware that she was going to change them if they were wrong. It seems likely that she wanted to be seen to get a high mark. I couldn't say how many other children, if any, behaved like this, but it does suggest that pupil-marked tests were probably not a reliable form of assessment. In many cases, marks were likely to be over-estimates. An exception to this was Darren. Darren was quite enthusiastic about mental arithmetic, but was not good at looking after his equipment. On more than one occasion, I noticed that Darren missed the first question in a test because he did not have a pencil.

Preparing for external tests

On the whole, the children did not do practice tests or questions though they were sometimes asked to carry out tasks in ways that the teachers hoped might help with the tests. The teachers were well aware that the tests were likely to contain mathematics the children could not do and to present reading problems. Some of the teachers showed concern that even if the children could read the questions and were able to do the mathematics, they might not be able to work out what was required or they might not follow the instructions exactly. As the time for tests approached, such issues were mentioned more frequently:

> A worksheet on fractions was given out. The teacher went through the sheet question by question, emphasising exactly what the children had to do and how they had to record the answers. He explained that they needed to do their 'best work'. He then went on to talk about a similar sheet the children had done the previous day. Some children had done the wrong thing. For example, one child had drawn a triangle when asked to draw a circle. One had coloured half a shape when asked to colour a quarter. The teacher reiterated the need to read instructions carefully and to do exactly what was asked.

The use of the phrase 'best work' in this incident suggests that the teacher put great emphasis on correct completion of tasks. As was shown in the last chapter, some of the children completing fraction tasks incorrectly showed good understanding of the mathematical ideas involved in their spoken comments. This seemed to lead to frustration on the teacher's part, as he knew that he was under pressure to prepare children for the standard written tests and that their results on these tests might not reflect their understanding. There was a need for tangible evidence of what the children could do, both in the form of test answers and correctly completed written tasks. Some children seemed anxious to do what was required but did not always seem to be able to work out what this was. Other children, such as Wesley and Darren, seemed less concerned about doing exactly what they were told, as the incident at the start of this chapter illustrates.

External tests

Many of the questions in the external tests contained mathematics the children had never met. Some presented reading difficulties and a few also required answers to be written in words. The test regulations did allow help with reading and writing, although the adults seemed to have mixed views about this. I did not see the tests taking place, so was unable to see where the help was given but I did see some of the papers afterwards. An example of a child having difficulty with a question involving reading and writing is given here:

> I looked at Christopher's answer to a question on the Year 5 optional test. The question, shown in Figure 9.2, required the children to make the largest number possible with the digits 5, 0, 8 and 2 and to write the number in words. Christopher correctly made the largest possible answer and wrote it in figures as 8520. However, he had difficulty writing the number in words. He actually wrote, 'eint fifor tow zirower'. Christopher received no marks for his answer to this question because he had not written the number in words in the way required.

Christopher's answer raises two slightly different but related issues. The first is that the tests present problems for children with reading and writing difficulties and they may lose marks as a result. In fact, even if Christopher's answer had been accepted as eight five two zero incorrectly spelt he would not have received a mark because he had missed out 'thousand' and 'hundred'. The second issue is that many of the questions are worth only one mark and thus children giving partially correct answers, as Christopher did, will gain no marks. I looked through some papers where children had been partly right on several questions but had not been awarded a mark for any of them. From Christopher's answer it appears that he was able to read and understand the question. Many children left out questions, possibly

Look at these digits.

5   0   8   2

Make the **largest number possible** with the digits.

Write your number in **words**.

....

Figure 9.2 Digits question from Year 5 mathematics test

because of reading difficulties. Sometimes, children's answers suggested that they had not read the question exactly. An example is Sean, who may have had difficulty in reading the question or may have answered it in a hurry:

> I looked at Sean's answer to a question about fractions, shown in Figure 9.3. The question asked, 'What fraction of these tiles is circled?' In the space for the answer, Sean had written the word 'squares'.

Sean had clearly not answered the question which had been asked. Presumably, he thought the question was asking what shapes rather than what fraction. He did correctly identify the shapes but received no marks. I came across other examples of children failing to gain marks in this way because they had not answered the question that had been asked, although they had written something that was mathematically correct. This question is interesting for another reason. Sean's set had spent a great deal of time on fractions, as related in earlier chapters. This question was one of a fairly small number on the paper that they might have a realistic chance of answering from what they had been taught. I was able to look at thirteen papers and only two of them had correctly answered this question. Possibly, this was because the question was slightly different from those they were used to as it dealt with fractions of a set of objects rather than fractions of a shape. Perhaps the reading required was too much or the children simply could not work out what was required. Many of them gave no answer to this question.

What fraction of these tiles are circled?

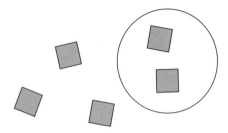

Figure 9.3 Fractions question from Year 5 mathematics test

Sean gained 8 marks out of the 61 possible in the test. The children needed to score 15 marks to achieve Level 3, the lowest level that could be awarded from this test. The booklet accompanying the test confirms that Sean's score puts him in the bottom fifth of his age group. I did not see all the results for Sean's set but was able to see a full list of results for one set I worked with. The children were starting Year 5 and their results from the test taken in Year 4 (QCA 1999d) were shown. Of the eighteen children who did the written test, half were recorded as below Level 2, the lowest level possible on the test. The other half did achieve Level 2 with the highest mark being 18 out of a possible 59. Mental arithmetic scores were also given for seventeen of the children. Only three of the children scored more than 5 out of 20, with the highest mark being 7. One child, Stacey, scored no marks at all.

As far as I was aware, little use was made of this information about test scores. Normally, the results merely presented confirmation that these children were unsuccessful compared to others of the same age. However, there were a few exceptions. For example, Bob did relatively well in his Year 5 test and, along with others in his set, got higher marks than some children in higher sets. This had started a discussion about whether some children should be moved or whether the setting system should be modified to give parallel groups.

Discussion

The role of other adults

My observations suggest that in one of the classes, the presence of other adults had an effect on assessment in terms of making decisions about teaching and learning. For example, in the 'coins in the jar' and similar incidents, the combined views of the adults were used to inform decisions about what might be done immediately, or in subsequent lessons, or how activities might be altered. The combined views of the adults were also sometimes used to consider the strengths and difficulties of individuals, usually in discussions outside the lesson. The success of this team in considering and acting on pupil difficulties is notable as these areas are highlighted in recent reports as things teachers are finding difficult. For example, one evaluation of the implementation of the Numeracy Strategy suggests some teachers have difficulty in diagnosing and responding to individual differences in pupil understanding (Earl *et al.* 2001). A similar point is made in another evaluation of the Numeracy Strategy (OFSTED 2001) which talks about the need to move from noticing pupils' responses to acting upon them, perhaps in subsequent lessons. It is further suggested that diagnosing and subsequently addressing pupils' misunderstandings are the key to higher standards. It seems that the team of adults in the case study are able to focus on an aspect of teaching that many teachers are finding difficult to address. However, even though this team seemed relatively successful in carrying out day-to-day assessment, there were problems. The team sometimes discussed the fact that pupils performed inconsistently and that it was very difficult to say categorically whether pupils could or could not do something.

Medium-term assessment

I shall use 'medium-term assessment' to cover all those assessments based on particular tasks aimed at reaching judgements rather than just arising as part of teaching. I saw many such forms of assessment, including short tests, individual assessment by adults, individual reciting of tables and worksheets for assessment purposes. All these presented problems. The most fundamental problem seemed to be just how accurate and consistent the child needed to be before it could be said that they 'can do' a particular thing. My findings tend to support the view of Watson (2001) that we cannot say for certain what pupils can do. All the methods of assessment I observed seemed to carry problems for particular pupils. Sometimes the method of assessment did not suit the pupil, sometimes it appeared that pupils either consciously or subconsciously were declining to co-operate with certain forms of assessment.

Often it was only possible to speculate what was going wrong.

Douglas may have been assessed on a particularly bad day for him for personal reasons, he may have been tired because it was the end of term or he may simply not have seen the point in answering the questions put. Sean performed poorly on the sheet about multiplying by 4, suggesting perhaps that assessment of simple items presented in a similar way was not appropriate for him. However, the formal assessment consisted of a variety of harder items presented in different ways. He fared no better on this. Perhaps my informal assessment of Sean's understanding based on his mental performance and informal remarks was over-optimistic. Perhaps by the end of the year Sean was not committed to performing well on assessment, however it was presented. Although Sean appeared to lose interest in getting high marks, Penny seemed determined to do so. The fact that she claimed a test score which was not 'true' may have made little difference to her learning. Perhaps more important was that in order to do this she withdrew from any serious discussion of questions she had misunderstood as I suspected Matthew did on a previous occasion. This relates to the concern raised by Black (1999) about the balance between the marking function and the learning function of assessment.

External tests

At first glance, it is difficult to see what was gained by asking these children to sit external tests, as there were very few questions they could do. In discussing test questions, Clausen-May (2001) suggests that tests should not include too many questions which are easy. She suggests that a question which nearly all pupils can do does not help to distinguish between the majority of pupils. As far as most of the pupils I worked with are concerned, this is a no-win situation. If tests are deliberately written so that not all pupils succeed on them, then these are the pupils most likely to fail. The statistical information presented with the tests about comparisons with other pupils and likely pupil progress was similarly negative. It was not surprising that most of the teachers were unhappy about the tests and in the school where the option existed, the special needs class did not take the tests. However, they did have some possible positive consequences. For example, Bob did relatively well on the tests and appeared to have made good progress over the year. His performance and the fact that others in his set out-performed children in different sets led the teachers to question how children were placed. In the school where the special needs children did not sit the test, none of them had the opportunity to demonstrate that they could perform as well as other children.

Responding to assessment

My findings suggest that all forms of assessment were problematic and that it was difficult to reach firm conclusions. This posed a dilemma for teachers in deciding what to do next. In particular, if pupils could not do something consistently and accurately, the teachers were faced with choices about whether to move on or back and whether to revise or revisit certain aspects. This issue will be discussed in more detail in the final chapter.

Classroom suggestions

Observing and listening

Observing and listening are themselves forms of assessment. As well as listening for particular strengths and difficulties or to see if the main points of the lesson appear to be understood, there are also some general issues about observing and listening which need to be considered:

- How much interpretation is involved in arriving at a judgement from an observation?
- Do other adults in the classroom have the opportunity to pass their observations on to the teacher?
- Should some observations and comments be acted upon immediately? If so, who makes this decision?

There are some particular things that adults might look and listen for during teaching and learning. Such observation might also be instructive during more formal types of assessment such as classroom tests or external tests. In particular, adults might look and listen for the following:

- Does the child appear to understand the main points of the lesson or the activity?
- Does the child appear to have any particular difficulty that needs addressing quickly?
- Does the child make any comments that suggest particular understanding or interest or which relate to aspects not yet taught?

- Under what circumstances does the child seem to give particularly positive answers?
- Under what circumstances does the child seem to give weaker answers or do answers seem to become less accurate?
- Are children doing classroom tests showing signs of arriving at the answers themselves?
- Are children working on written assessment tasks showing signs of boredom, disengagement or anxiety?

Planning and teaching

Although assessment is an inevitable part of teaching, there is a question about how much assessment needs to take place and whether this can have a demoralising effect on adults and children. Some decisions need to be made in the light of why teachers are assessing. The need for standardised judgements may lead to particular types of assessment. A desire to discover what children seem to be able to do and understand mathematically under optimum conditions is likely to lead to a different style of assessment. Teachers also have decisions to make about the use of informal and formal tests, though increasingly such decisions are not always left in the hands of individual teachers. Here are some issues to consider:

- Is the balance between new ideas and assessment reasonable or are assessment activities dominating?
- If classroom tests are given, how important are the marks and should they be shared publicly?
- How important is the discussion of answers after classrooms tests? If it is important, are all children encouraged to participate?
- If external tests are used, is full advantage taken of the concessions allowed for pupils with particular needs?
- If external tests are not taken, is there any other mechanism for considering whether children are correctly placed in sets or groups and whether they do have genuine difficulties?

10 Conclusion

It was the last week of the summer term and the final day of my field-work. I walked from the classroom with the teacher and we chatted about some of the children; in particular, we talked about Damian. We agreed Damian had made progress over the year and had shown mathematical strengths on some occasions. Despite this, the teacher was frustrated at not really understanding 'the reason' for Damian's difficulties or knowing 'the solution'. I sympathised with the teacher. Although I had tried to gain some understanding of Damian's mathematical strengths and weaknesses and of what helped and hindered him, I knew I was not in a position to talk with any conviction about a simple 'reason' or 'solution'.

Introduction

The picture presented by my research is complex and occasionally contradictory. However, there were some findings arising from my observation. In this chapter I will start by discussing these and will move on to discuss some issues which they raise. Finally, I will talk about what might be done to help the children I worked with and others like them.

I believe that the findings are supported by evidence from all four sets. Despite their similarities, the sets also had some marked differences. This was an important aspect of the research, not because it was intended as a comparison of approaches or schools or teachers, but rather because I wanted to look for messages which arose in more than one situation. I invite those who work in similar situations to consider whether they believe these findings are also applicable there.

My research has some obvious limitations. For example, it is not possible to tell from this research whether low-attaining students in mixed-ability classes would behave in the same way. Similarly, although aspects of the findings may apply more widely, to what extent some or all of my findings might apply to children who are not classified as low attainers is currently unclear.

Findings

Nothing works for everyone

Although I saw many children being successful at mathematics as well as some having difficulties, I saw no one thing that led to success for everyone. Some children had difficulties with aspects of mathematics teaching which were well established in English primary schools but have recently been called into question. This included difficulties with standard algorithms and written methods. However, I also saw some children experiencing difficulties with aspects such as number lines, mental methods or non-standard methods of calculation. At the time of the research, many of these were regarded as being more helpful than methods used in the past. It is possible that they were helpful to many children, but they certainly did not help everybody.

My initial study of the four boys I called the whisperers suggests that there were certain things that suited them, such as mental calculations and challenging work. There were other things that did not suit them such as formal algorithms and simple repetitive work. These factors were the same for some other children I met, but not all. Claire worked best on written tasks, Julie showed a preference for formal algorithms. Nevertheless, all these children were similar in that they had marked preferences which influenced how well they did on any given task.

Sometimes it was easy to appreciate why certain approaches hindered or helped certain children. For example, Damian appeared to have perceptual difficulties, which meant that number lines and other forms of diagram were unlikely to help him. Sometimes it was less logical, for example James often preferred to use practical equipment despite his physical difficulties in handling it. Sometimes it took adults a long time to work out what worked best for an individual, or it never became clear. Possibly some of the children could have answered this themselves.

Children can surprise us

The comments made by the whisperers show that children sometimes say or do something which is mathematically surprising. Although these four boys first highlighted this issue, it was raised over and over again by observation of different children during the research. Sometimes children did surprisingly well when working in a way that seemed to suit them. A clear example of this was Douglas working with technology. Often, positive surprises came in response to a non-standard piece of mathematics which might well have been harder than usual. Examples of this include Penny's enthusiasm for concave shapes, Wesley's work on equivalent fractions and Miriam's discussion of leap years. However, surprises were not always easy to explain in this way.

Most maths tasks can be difficult

Although this book contains many examples of children reacting positively to mathematics, it also (unsurprisingly) contains many examples of them having difficulties. From the point of view of adults, much of the mathematics the children worked on would appear to be extremely simple. Nevertheless, for some of the children it presented great difficulties. In particular, in many cases children experienced problems with mathematics which was apparently much easier than that officially assigned to their age group. At the time this research was carried out, it was very clearly stated what children of a given age should be able to do. In a sense, this contributed to a sense of failure and was a constant reminder that the children were not working at the level they were 'supposed' to be at.

Performance can be inconsistent

The two sections above about surprise and difficulty may seem to contradict each other, but actually were consistent messages throughout the research. I saw many examples of difficulties as well as examples of positive surprises. Often, both things came from the same children. As has been discussed above, this could sometimes be explained in terms of the way the task was presented or the interest or difficulty of the task. However, these explanations only went a small way towards explaining the many inconsistencies I saw. Often, inconsistencies arose when looking at small things like recall of particular facts or the ability to count. Often, children gave a different answer to the same question on a different day or in different circumstances. Sometimes they gave a different answer to a question repeated on the same day and in the same way.

Issues arising

Responding to inconsistencies

The inconsistencies discussed above raise the important issue of what teachers and other adults do in response to this situation. One question which seemed to be ever-present in the classrooms was to what extent ideas should be repeated and revised. The adults talked about when it was important to go back and do something similar and when it was best to move forward or on to something different. Decisions about these things were constrained by the systems within the schools, but it is likely that they were also influenced by the teachers' views about the children concerned and about mathematics.

All of the children were considered to be low attainers as far as mathematics was concerned. This may have influenced the teachers' actions when children performed inconsistently, with a tendency for them to assume that the children did not really understand or could not really do something and hence more practice was needed. It is possible that inconsistent answers given by children considered to be higher attainers might be put down to 'silly mistakes' or 'careless slips' and they might be allowed to progress to harder ideas.

Views of mathematics

Responses to inconsistencies are also likely to be influenced by views about mathematics. A widespread view is that mathematical learning is hierarchical and it is impossible to learn a particular step without first knowing the easier steps it depends on. Such a view means that teachers are likely to make a decision to go back over material until it is mastered before moving on.

In fact, the whole idea of mastery is problematic. Some of the teachers seemed to have an ideal where children had 'mastered' a particular idea and hence would always get every example right, however that idea was presented. In the classrooms I was in, this never happened. Some children mostly got things right, some presented a much more mixed picture, while a few only got things wrong in particular circumstances such as when they couldn't read or understand the words involved. No one got everything right all the time. This perfection was what was looked for as a sign that a child might need harder work or even be moved to a higher set, but it never happened. It could be argued that this confirmed that all the children were correctly placed and none were being given work that was too easy. This is not supported by what happened when work of different levels of difficulty was presented. Some children who made occasional mistakes continued to do so when much easier work was presented. An example of this was Michael making a mistake in counting a row of Smarties. Sometimes, as with Sean and Wesley, children actually showed *poorer* performance when work got easier.

Beyond mathematics

Throughout my research, I tried to be sensitive to the way the class-rooms operated and the pressures on the teachers and children. Nevertheless, my focus was always mathematical. My data consisted largely of children's responses to mathematical tasks, including many routine tasks. One question my work raises is whether explanations about children's strengths and difficulties can be given in terms of mathematics alone. I became increasingly doubtful that this was the case. For example, it was not possible to talk about Sean's sheet about multiplying by 4 purely in terms of whether he knew the 4 times table, as the sheet gave contradictory information about this. Any considerations of children's performance are likely to be more meaningful if they also consider non-mathematical aspects such as whether the children are motivated or bored by a task, whether they are able to access the task and how they wish to be perceived by their friends. I was hoping that factual mathematical information would give me a good picture of the children's mathematics. Actually, I came to regard such information as highly suspect since personal, psychological and social contexts all played important roles. This is particularly alarming given the importance the assessment system in use at the time attached to such information and the central place of assessment in teaching.

Possible ways forward

The preceding chapters all contain suggestions about what adults might look and listen for and do in certain situations, though it is not claimed that they will all help all children. At first glance it is hard to see what the suggestions have in common, or how they can easily be summarised. I would suggest that the common feature is that the teaching and planning suggestions link to the observing and listening suggestions and both relate to my observations. Where I saw teachers moving children forward, it was often because their actions were based on detailed observation and trying to find ways of responding to the situation. The reality of working in these classrooms seemed to be in accepting that things would not always go smoothly first time, but that every effort would be made to respond to difficulties. This was a job that called for patience, inventiveness and energy from teachers and classroom assistants. As the comments about Damian at the start of this chapter illustrate, it remained a complex job right till the end of the school year, rather than something that was suddenly 'solved'.

There are some other general messages from my research. One piece of advice would be to listen for the whispers. My experience was that in listening carefully I heard many positive things. I believe this is likely to be the case wherever children are allowed, or preferably encouraged, to speak while doing mathematics. Individual chapters have already made suggestions about what adults might listen for in different circumstances. The crucial point about whispering to me was that it sometimes gave a completely different and more positive view of children's mathematical understanding. Teachers are clearly not in a position to ignore the way children respond to formal tasks, but they may supplement their views of children by taking into account their informal comments. As strengths are identified, they too can be considered in planning ways forward.

My second piece of advice concerns the other theme of this book, that of the maths fairy. The idea that one day the fairy would deliver sudden mathematical success to the children was a private adult joke. However, the sudden success was sometimes very real, though sadly not sustained. The important thing is that children were offered opportunities to do things slightly harder or more unusual. They did not always take these opportunities, but they sometimes did. On the other hand, simplifying tasks and repeating ideas did not seem to me to be as successful as some teachers hoped it would be. All of this means that there is a case for sometimes moving on and sometimes taking risks. The children may surprise you.

My advice, like my findings, may appear to be contradictory, but it is rather a case of a combined approach. Responding to the children and acting in a way that is designed to address their weaknesses and build on their strengths are vital. Such an approach will be familiar to adults with experience in similar settings. In addition, I believe there is a place for including some harder mathematical ideas which there is no guarantee the children will be able to cope with.

Beyond the classrooms

Some suggestions are now made to policy-makers, concerning rewards systems and assessment regimes. I have tried to point to the complexities of life in bottom sets and the complex job facing the adults that work there. This should be borne in mind when considering policies which reward teachers of higher-attaining pupils and schools with a small percentage of low attainers. Another issue worth considering is that many of the adults I worked alongside were classroom assistants, who often suffer from low pay and poor conditions of service. Despite this, they were often faced with the difficult job of trying to work out what to try out next when working alongside children who were not responding to the initial approach. I believe attitudes to assessment fostered by the existing testing regime also impacted on what I saw in the classrooms. In particular, concerns about making sure children could do something if tested or could continue to do the same thing with accuracy appeared to hold back both teachers and children.

Bibliography

Ainley, J. (1991) 'Is there any mathematics in measurement?', in D. Pimm and E. Love (eds) *Teaching and Learning School Mathematics*, London: Hodder & Stoughton.

Ainley, J. (1996) *Enriching Primary Mathematics with IT*, London: Hodder & Stoughton.

Alam, S., Curtis, B., Garner, S., MacAdams, C., Pike, G., Roberts, W. with Maple, L. (1994) *A Feel for Number: Activities for Number Recovery Programmes*, London: BEAM.

Allebone, B. (1998) 'Providing for able children in the primary classroom', *Education 3–13*, 26(1): 64–69.

Anghileri, J. (2000) *Teaching Number Sense*, London: Continuum.

Anghileri, J. (2001) 'Contrasting approaches that challenge tradition', in J. Anghileri (ed.) *Principles and Practices in Arithmetic Teaching*, Buckingham: Open University Press.

Anghileri, J., Beishuizen, M. and Van Putten, K. (2002) 'From informal strategies to structured procedures: mind the gap!', *Educational Studies in Mathematics*, 49: 149–170.

Aplin, R. (1998) *Assisting Numeracy: A Handbook for Classroom Assistants*, London: BEAM.

Askew, M. (2001) 'Policy, practices and principles in teaching numeracy: what makes a difference?', in P. Gates (ed.) *Issues in Mathematics Teaching*, London: RoutledgeFalmer.

Askew, M., Bibby, T. and Brown, M. (1997) *Raising Attainment in Primary Numeracy: Final Report*, London: King's College.

Askew, M., Briscoe, R., Ebbutt, S., Maple, L. and Mosley, F. (1996) *Number at Key Stage 2: Core Materials for Teaching and Assessing Number and Algebra*, London: BEAM.

Bailey, K. D. (1978) *Methods of Social Research*, London: Collier-Macmillan.

Bauersfeld, H. (1995) '"Language games" in the mathematics classroom: their function and their effects', in P. Cobb. and H. Bauersfeld (eds) *The Emergence of Mathematical Meaning: Interaction in Classroom Cultures*, Hillsdale, NJ: Lawrence Erlbaum Associates.

BECTa (2001) 'Calculator activities for primary schools from Becta', *Micromath*, 17(3): 19–34.

Beishuizen, M. (1993) 'Mental strategies and materials or models for addition and subtraction up to 101 in Dutch second grades', *Journal for Research in Mathematics Education*, 24(4): 294–323.

Bennett, N., Desforges, C., Cockburn, A. and Wilkinson, B. (1984) *The Quality of Pupil Learning Experiences*, London: Lawrence Erlbaum Associates.

Bierhoff, H. (1996) *Laying the Foundations of Numeracy: A Comparison of Primary School Textbooks in Britain, Germany and Switzerland*, London: National Institute of Economic and Social Research.

Black, P. (1999) 'Assessment, learning theories and testing systems', in P. Murphy (ed.) *Learners, Learning and Assessment*, London: Paul Chapman Publishing in association with the Open University.

Black, P. J. (1998) *Testing: Friend or Foe? Theory and Practice of Assessment and Testing*, London: Falmer Press.

Boaler, J. (1997) 'Setting, social class and survival of the quickest', *British Educational Research Journal*, 23(5): 575–595.

Boaler, J., Wiliam, D. and Brown, M. (2000) 'Students' experiences of ability grouping – disaffection, polarisation and the construction of failure', *British Educational Research Journal*, 26(5): 631–648.

Bramald, R. (2000) 'Introducing the empty numberline, the Dutch approach to teaching numberskills', *Education 3–13*, 28: 5–12.

Brissenden, T. (1988) *Talking about Mathematics: Mathematical Discussions in Primary Classrooms*, Oxford: Basil Blackwell.

Brown, M. (1999) 'Swings of the pendulum', in I. Thompson (ed.) *Issues in Teaching Numeracy in Primary Schools*, Buckingham: Open University Press.

Brown, M. (2001) 'Influences on the teaching of number in England', in J. Anghileri (ed.) *Principles and Practices in Arithmetic Teaching*, Buckingham: Open University Press.

Chinn, S. (1996) *What to Do When You Can't Learn the Times Tables*, Baldock: Egon Publishers.

Clausen-May, T. (2001) *An Approach to Test Development*, Slough: NFER.

Cobb, P. and Yackel, E. (1998) 'A constructivist perspective on the culture of the mathematics classroom', in F. Seeger, J. Voigt and U. Waschescio (eds) *The Culture of the Mathematics Classroom*, Cambridge: Cambridge University Press.

Cockburn, A. (1999) *Teaching Mathematics with Insight: The Identification, Diagnosis and Remediation of Young Children's Mathematical Errors*, London: Falmer Press.

Cockcroft, W. H. (1982) *Mathematics Counts: Report of the Committee of Inquiry into the Teaching of Mathematics in Schools*, London: HMSO.

Croll, P. and Moses, D. (2000) *Special Needs in the Primary School*, London: Cassell.

Denvir, B. and Brown, M. (1986) 'Understanding of number concepts in low attaining 7–9 year olds: Part 2, the teaching studies', *Educational Studies in Mathematics*, 17: 143–164.

Denvir, B., Stolz, C. and Brown, M. (1982) *Low Attainers in Mathematics 5–16: Policies and Practices in Schools*, London: Methuen Educational.

DES (1989) *Mathematics in the National Curriculum*, London: HMSO.

DfEE (1998) *Numeracy Matters: The Preliminary Report of the Numeracy Task Force*, London: DfEE Publications.

DfEE (1999a) *The National Numeracy Strategy: Framework for Teaching Mathematics from Reception to Year 6*, Sudbury: DfEE Publications.

DfEE (1999b) *The National Numeracy Strategy: Mathematical Vocabulary*, Sudbury: DfEE Publications.

DfEE and QCA (1999) *Mathematics: The National Curriculum for England*, Norwich: The Stationery Office.

DfES (2001) *The National Numeracy Strategy: Guidance to Support Pupils with Specific Needs in the Daily Mathematics Lesson*, Sudbury: DfES Publications.

Dobson, J. and Henthorne, K. (1999) *Pupil Mobility in Schools*, London: DfEE Publications.

Durkin, K. (1991) 'Language in mathematical education: an introduction', in K. Durkin and B. Shire (eds) *Language in Mathematical Education: Research and Practice*, Milton Keynes: Open University Press.

Durkin, K. and Shire, B. (1991) 'Lexical ambiguity in mathematical contexts', in K. Durkin and B. Shire (eds) *Language in Mathematical Education, Research and Practice*, Milton Keynes: Open University Press.

Earl, L., Levin, B., Leithwood, K., Fullan, M., Watson, N. with Torrance, N., Jantzi, D. and Mascall, B. (2001) *Watching and Learning 2: OISE/UT Evaluation of the Implementation of the National Literacy and Numeracy Strategies*, Toronto: Ontario Institute for Studies in Education, University of Toronto.

Farell, P., Balshaw, M. and Polat, F. (1999) *The Management, Role and Training of Learning Support Assistants: Teachers and Assistants Working Together*, Nottingham: DfEE Publications.

Fielker, D. (1997) 'Some notes on mental mathematics', *Mathematics Teaching*, 160: 9–11.

Fox, B., Montague-Smith, A. and Wilkes, S. (2000) *Using ICT in Primary Mathematics: Practice and Possibilities*, London: David Fulton Publishers.

Fox, G. (1998) *A Handbook for Learning Support Assistants: Teachers and Assistants Working Together*, London: David Fulton Publishers.

Gamoran, A. (1993) 'Alternative uses of ability grouping in secondary schools: Can we bring high-quality instruction to low-ability classes?' *American Journal of Education*, 102: 1–22.

Ginsburg, H. (1977) *Children's Arithmetic: The Learning Process*, New York: D. Van Nostrand Company.

Gray, E. M. (1991) 'An analysis of diverging approaches to simple arith-

metic: preference and its consequences', *Educational Studies in Mathematics*, 22: 551–574.

Hall, D. (2001) *Assessing the Needs of Bilingual Pupils: Living in Two Languages* (2nd edn), London: David Fulton Publishers.

Harries, T. and Spooner, M. (2000) *Mental Mathematics for the Numeracy Hour*, London: David Fulton Publishers.

Harries, T. and Sutherland, R. (1999) 'Primary school mathematics textbooks: an international comparison', in I. Thompson (ed.) *Issues in Teaching Numeracy in Primary Schools*, Buckingham: Open University Press.

Hart, K. (1989) 'Place value: subtraction', in D. C. Johnson (ed.) *Children's Mathematical Frameworks 8–13: A Study of Classroom Teaching*, Nottingham: The Shell Centre.

Hart, S. (1996) *Beyond Special Needs, Enhancing Children's Learning through Innovative Thinking*, London: Paul Chapman Publishing.

Haylock, D. (1991) *Teaching Mathematics to Low Attainers, 8–12*, London: Paul Chapman Publishing.

Houssart, J. (1999) 'Teachers' perceptions of good tasks in primary mathematics', *British Society for Research into Learning Mathematics*, Proceedings of the Day Conference held at the Open University, Saturday, 27 February.

Houssart, J. (2000) 'I haven't used them yet', *Micromath*, 16(2): 14–17.

Houssart, J. (2001a) 'Setting tasks and setting children', paper presented at the Fifth British Congress of Mathematics Education, Keele University, 5–7 July.

Houssart, J. (2001b) 'Counting difficulties at Key Stage Two', *Support for Learning*, 16(1): 11–16.

Houssart, J. (2001c) 'Rival classroom discourses and inquiry mathematics: "The Whisperers"', *For the Learning of Mathematics*, 21(3): 2–8.

Houssart, J. (2002a) 'Count me out: task refusal in primary mathematics', *Support for Learning*, 17(2): 75–79.

Houssart, J. (2002b) 'Simplification and repetition of mathematical tasks: a recipe for success or failure?' *Journal of Mathematical Behaviour*, 21: 191–202.

Hughes, M. (1986) *Children and Number: Difficulties in Learning Mathematics*, Oxford: Blackwell.

Ireson, J. and Hallam, S. (2001) *Ability Grouping in Education*, London: Paul Chapman Publishing.

Liebeck, P. (1984) *How Children Learn Mathematics: A Guide for Parents and Teachers*, London: Penguin Books.

Low Attainers in Mathematics Project (1987) *Better Mathematics: A Curriculum Development Study*, London: HMSO.

Martino, A. M. and Maher, C. A. (1999) 'Teacher questioning to promote justification and generalisation in mathematics: what research practice taught us', *Journal of Mathematical Behaviour*, 18(1): 53–78.

Mathematical Association (1987) *Calculator Investigations*, Leicester: Mathematical Association.

Mathematical Association (1992) *Mental Methods in Mathematics: A First Resort*, Leicester: Mathematical Association.

Menne, J. (2001) 'Jumping ahead: an innovative teaching programme', in J. Anghileri (ed.) *Principles and Practices in Arithmetic Teaching*, Buckingham: Open University Press.

Merttens, R. (1996) 'Primary maths in crisis: what is to be done?', in R. Merttens (ed.) *Teaching Numeracy: Maths in the Primary Classroom*, Leamington Spa: Scholastic.

Millett, A. and Johnson, D. C. (1996) 'Solving teachers' problems? The role of the commercial mathematics scheme', in D. Johnson and A. Millett (eds) *Implementing the Mathematics National Curriculum: Policy, Politics and Practice*, London: Paul Chapman Publishing.

Moyer, P. S. (2001) 'Are we having fun yet? How teachers use manipulatives to teach mathematics', *Educational Studies in Mathematics*, 47: 175–197.

NCET (1997) *Primary Mathematics with IT*, Coventry: National Council for Educational Technology.

Nuffield Mathematics Project (1967) *I Do and I Understand*, London: W&R Chambers and John Murray.

Oakes, J. (1990) *Multiplying Inequalities: the effects of race, social class and tracking on opportunities to learn mathematics and science*, Santa Monica: RAND.

OFSTED (1993) *The Teaching and Learning of Number in Primary Schools*, HMSO.

OFSTED (1994) *Science and Mathematics in Schools: a review*, HMSO.

OFSTED (1998) *Setting in Primary Schools*, London: OFSTED Publications.

OFSTED (2000) *The National Numeracy Strategy: An interim evaluation by HMI*, London: Office for Standards in Education.

OFSTED (2001) *The National Numeracy Strategy: The second year, an evaluation by HMI*, London: Office for Standards in Education.

OFSTED (2002) *Managing Pupil Mobility*, London: OFSTED Publications.

Ollerton, M. (2003) *Everyone is Special*, Derby: Association of Teachers of Mathematics.

Open University (1982) *PM 537: Calculators in the Primary School*, Milton Keynes: The Open University.

Page, R. N. (1989) 'The lower track curriculum at Heavenly high school: cycles of prejudice', *Journal of Curriculum Studies*, 21: 197–221.

Pimm, D. (1987) *Speaking Mathematically*, London: Routledge & Kegan Paul.

QCA (1998a) *Standards at Key Stage 2 English, Mathematics and Science: Report on the 1997 National Curriculum Assessments for 11-Year-Olds*, Sudbury: QCA Publications.

QCA (1998b) *Year 5 English and Mathematics Test: Teacher's Guide*, Sudbury: QCA Publications.

QCA (1999a) *The National Numeracy Strategy: Teaching Mental Calculation Strategies*, Sudbury: QCA Publications.

QCA (1999b) *The National Numeracy Strategy: Teaching Written Calculations, Guidance for Teachers at Key Stages 1 and 2*, Sudbury: QCA Publications.

QCA (1999c) *Standards in Mathematics: Exemplification of Key Learning Objectives*, Sudbury: QCA Publications.

QCA (1999d) *Year 4 Mathematics Test: Mathematics Booklet*, Sudbury: QCA Publications.

QCA (2000) *Standards at Key Stage 2 English, Mathematics and Science: Report on the 1999 National Curriculum Assessments for 11-Year-Olds*, Sudbury: QCA Publications.

Robbins, B. (2000) *Inclusive Mathematics 5–11*, London: Continuum.

Rousham, L. and Rowland, T. (1996) 'Numeracy and calculators', in R. Merttens (ed.) *Teaching Numeracy: Maths in the Primary Classroom*, Lemington Spa: Scholastic.

Rowland, T. (1994) *CAN in Suffolk: The First Six Months of a Calculator-Aware Number Curriculum*, Cambridge: Homerton College.

Ruthven, K. (1999) 'The pedagogy of calculator use', in I. Thompson (ed.) *Issues in Teaching Numeracy in Primary Schools*, Buckingham: Open University Press.

Ruthven, K. (2001) 'The English experience of a calculator-aware number curriculum', in J. Anghileri (ed.) *Principles and Practices in Arithmetic Teaching: Innovative Approaches for the Primary Classroom*, Buckingham: Open University Press.

Ruthven, K. and Chaplin, D. (1997) 'The calculator as a cognitive tool: upper primary pupils tackling a realistic number problem', *International Journal of Computers for Mathematical Learning*, 2(2): 93–124.

SCAA (1993) *Evaluation of the Implementation of National Curriculum Mathematics at Key Stages 1, 2 and 3*, vol. 1: *Report*, London: School Curriculum and Assessment Authority.

SCAA (1997) *The Use of Calculators at Key Stages 1–3*, Middlesex: SCAA Publications.

Seeger, F. (1998) 'Representations in the mathematics classroom: reflections and constructions', in F. Seeger, J. Voigt and U. Waschescio (eds) *The Culture of the Mathematics Classroom*, Cambridge: Cambridge University Press.

Shuard, H. and Rothery, A. (1984) *Children Reading Mathematics*, London: John Murray.

Shuard, H., Walsh, A., Goodwin, J. and Worcester, V. (1991) *Calculators, Children and Mathematics*, London: Simon and Schuster.

Straker, A. (1999) 'The National Numeracy Project 1996–99', in I. Thompson (ed.) *Issues in Teaching Numeracy in Primary Schools*, Buckingham: Open University Press.

Sukhnandan, L. with Lee, B. (1998) *Streaming, Setting and Grouping by Ability: A Review of the Literature*, Slough: National Foundation for Educational Research.

Thompson, I. (1997) 'The early years number curriculum today', in I. Thompson (ed.) *Teaching and Learning Early Number*, Buckingham: Open University Press.

Thompson, I. (1999) 'Written methods of calculation', in I. Thompson (ed.) *Issues in Teaching Numeracy in Primary Schools*, Buckingham: Open University Press.

Trickett, L. and Sulke, F. (1988) 'Low attainers can do mathematics', in D. Pimm (ed.) *Mathematics, Teachers and Children*. London: Hodder & Stoughton.

Van den Heuvel-Panhuizen, M. (2001) 'Realistic mathematics education in the Netherlands', in J. Anghileri (ed.) *Principles and Practices in Arithmetic Teaching*, Buckingham: Open University Press.

Voigt, J. (1998) 'The culture of the mathematics classroom: negotiating the mathematical meaning of empirical phenomena', in F. Seeger, J. Voigt and U. Waschescio (eds) *The Culture of the Mathematics Classroom*, Cambridge: Cambridge University Press.

Watson, A. (1996) 'Teachers' notions of mathematical ability in their pupils', *Mathematics Education Review*, 8: 27–35.

Watson, A. (2001) 'Making judgements about pupils' mathematics', in P. Gates (ed.) *Issues in Mathematics Teaching*, London: RoutledgeFalmer.

Watson, A. and Mason, J. (1998) *Questions and Prompts for Mathematical Thinking*, Derby: Association of Teachers and Mathematics.

Whitburn, J. (2001) 'Pupil mobility and low attainment in mathematics', *Proceedings of the British Society for Research in to Learning Mathematics*, 21(1), Day conference held at the Manchester Metropolitan University, Saturday, 3 March.

Wiliam, D., Boaler, J. and Brown, M. (1999) 'We've still got to learn: low-attainers' experiences of setting', *Equals*, 5(1), 15–18.

Williams, E. M. and Shuard, H. (1970) *Primary Mathematics Today*, London: Longman.

Wood, D. (1988) *How Children Think and Learn*, Oxford: Basil Blackwell.

Wright, A. (1991) 'The assessment of bilingual pupils with reported learning difficulties', in T. Cline and N. Frederickson (eds) *Bilingual Pupils and the National Curriculum*, London: University College London.

Yackel, E. (2001) 'Perspectives on arithmetic from classroom-based research in the United States of America', in J. Anghileri (ed.) *Principles and Practices in Arithmetic Teaching*, Buckingham: Open University Press.

Index